Poetry for Peace of Mind

Poetry
for Peace of Mind

by Alison Wyrley Birch

Illustrations by Scott Cumming

❧ ❦

Doubleday & Company, Inc.
Garden City, New York
1978

Library of Congress Cataloging in Publication Data
Main entry under title:

Poetry for peace of mind.

1. American poetry. 2. English poetry.
3. Poetry—Therapeutic use. I. Birch, Alison Wyrley.
PS586.P58   821'.008
ISBN: 0-385-13253-0
Library of Congress Catalog Card Number 77-76959

Grateful acknowledgment is made for permission to include the following copyrighted material:

"A Vagrant" by Erik Axel Karlfeldt from *Anthology of Swedish Lyrics* translated by Charles Wharton Stork. Reprinted by permission of American-Scandinavian Foundation.

"On His Marks" by Richard Armour. Reprinted by permission of the author.

"Gee, You're So Beautiful That It's Starting to Rain" and "It's Raining in Love" excerpted from the book *The Pill Versus the Spring Hill Mine Disaster* by Richard Brautigan. Copyright © 1968 by Richard Brautigan. Reprinted by permission of Delacorte Press/Seymour Lawrence.

"Song of the Open Road," "Animals," "The Last Invocation," and "I Saw in Louisiana" from *Leaves of Grass* by Walt Whitman. Reprinted by permission of Doubleday & Company, Inc.

"Elegy for Jane," copyright 1950 by Theodore Roethke, "The Waking," copyright 1948 by Theodore Roethke, from *The Collected Poems of Theodore Roethke*. Reprinted by permission of Doubleday & Company, Inc.

"Time Does Not Bring Relief," "Song of a Second April," "Exiled," "Pity Me Not," "Eel Grass," "Recuerdo," "The Return," "God's World," "Afternoon on a Hill," "The Penitent," and "Travel" from *Collected Poems* by Edna St. Vincent Millay, Harper & Row. Copyright © 1917, 1921, 1922, 1923, 1934, 1945, 1948, 1950, 1951, 1962 by Edna St. Vincent Millay and Norma Millay (Ellis). Reprinted by permission of Norma Millay Ellis.

"Invictus" by William Ernest Henley from *Best Loved Poems of the American People* by Hazel Felleman. Reprinted by permission of Doubleday & Company, Inc.

"Two and the Sea" and "The Wordy People" by Jacqueline M. Fitzgerald. Reprinted by permission of the author.

"The Lovers" from *Cold Morning Sky* by Marya Zaturenska. Used with agreement of reprint publisher, Greenwood Press, Inc.

"Sonnet" from *Things of This World* by Richard Wilbur. Copyright © 1956 by Richard Wilbur. Reprinted by permission of Harcourt Brace Jovanovich, Inc.

#585, "I like to see it lap the miles," #288, "I'm nobody! Who are you?," #712, "Because I could not stop for Death," #1755, "To make a prairie it takes a clover and one bee," #47, "Heart! We will forget him!," #341, "After

CONTENTS

INTRODUCTION

Why Poetry?

The ancient Greeks knew what they were doing when they appointed Apollo as the god of both poetry and medicine. The healing power of poetry has been understood throughout time. Every emotional crisis, from love and birth to death and despair, has yielded in varying degrees to the poultice of poetry. Adolescents turn to poetry at that moment that is the bridge between childhood and maturity; and for every emotional crisis man can face, there is at least one poem that can bring healing.

"Poetry and medicine," said the poet-physician William Carlos Williams, "are the two parts of a whole."

"I've often thought," New York psychiatrist Jack J. Leedy has said, "that peptic ulcers, headaches, and many other diseases are really only poems, struggling to be born."

Psychiatrists, psychiatric social workers, and psychologists everywhere confess that they use poetry in their practice. At least two hundred hospitals for mentally ill people in the United States and Canada have poetry therapy groups meeting regularly—with amazing results.

The first formal poetry therapy group met in 1959 at the Mental Health Clinic at Brooklyn Cumberland Hospital. It was the brainchild of Dr. Leedy, Dr. Samuel Spector, and the late Eli Greifer. Then as now in structured poetry therapy groups, a mimeographed sheet containing several carefully selected poems was passed to each member of the group. Someone is elected to read the first poem. Poetry therapists are psychiatrically trained people, either doctors or social workers, who have had special training in the use of poetry with the mentally ill. When the poem has been read, the therapist asks, "How does it make you feel?" Without fail, the question triggers a discussion that couldn't have gotten off the ground without the poem.

Dr. Peter Luke of the Pilgrim State Hospital at Brentwood, Long Island, said, "A poem is a communication from the poet's unconscious and it gets right into the patient's unconscious. It's a valuable tool to get therapy going."

"The act of reading or writing a poem," said psychiatrist Robert E. Jones of the Institute of the Pennsylvania Hospital, "can provide a dignified release of emotion and also a direction, a form. The patient can say, 'I correspond with this poet'; for him, it's a personification, a step toward a sense of dignity."

I sat in on poetry therapy groups for about a year at Pilgrim State Hospital and watched poetry therapist Sidney Farcas work major miracles. One patient had been very withdrawn. He was thirty-nine years old and had been in the hospital for seventeen years. No form of therapy, none of the customary modalities, had produced a response from him in all that time. His stock reply to any question was, "It's none of my business." He was totally dependent on his mother and her decisions for him, and wouldn't even venture an objective opinion about his own life and condition. During the months I visited the groups, I saw incredible changes take place in him. He began to sit up straighter, to look people in the eye, and to talk objectively about his situation. I was there with the group the day he got angry. They had been reading "Invictus" by William Ernest Henley.

> Out of the night that covers me,
> Black as the pit from pole to pole,
> I thank whatever gods may be
> For my unconquerable soul.

In the fell clutch of circumstance
I have not winced nor cried aloud.
Under the bludgeonings of chance
My head is bloody, but unbowed.

Beyond this place of wrath and tears
Looms but the horror of the shade,
And yet the menace of the years
Finds and shall find me unafraid.

It matters not how strait the gate,
How charged with punishments the scroll,
I am the master of my fate:
I am the captain of my soul.

When they came to the last four lines, Warren blew up. "How can anyone here be master of his fate?" he asked, angrily. "They have bars on the windows and they don't allow me to smoke in my room."

"The restrictions the hospital places on you cause resentment," Sid Farcas said. "How about the restrictions your mother places on you?"

That was when Warren shouted, "I give up!" and walked out of the room. But he came back. He never missed a meeting, and from that day of his blowup he progressed steadily. He even telephoned his mother one day and asked to go home for the weekend, a heretofore unheard-of gesture of independence.

"We've seen no movement out of this hospital by Warren in seventeen years," Dr. Luke said. "We're looking for it now. Obviously," he added, "the tool of a poem shortens time. It's something like a miracle."

If poetry can work "something like a miracle" with a man whose life has been spent in an institution, the possibilities for solving the abstruse intricacies of the normal human condition are overwhelming. Poetry is a tremendously personal thing. It can't be injected into the blood stream or capsuled or bottled and ingested orally. Each poem has to happen to the individual. But mortals are strangely similar. Human conditions are much alike, and while one man's medicine may be another man's poison, it's much more apt to be his medicine also. With this hope in mind, I've sought out examples of poetry that might be prescribed for fifteen emotional problems nearly everyone has been familiar with at one time or another. These poems can be taken therapeutically, over and over again. Familiarity strengthens their effectiveness.

Only a few of the poems I've selected are "modern," because modern poetry often tends to instill emotional crisis rather than cure it. "Avoid modern poetry," poetry therapist–nurse Peggy Card of El Camino Hospital in California says emphatically. "So much of it is hostile, bitter, and despairing, it creates an atmosphere of uneasiness." Much modern poetry also requires too great an effort to understand. What we're looking for is that instantly recognizable poem that has a universal quality which will strike an answering response in the reader.

If you've never learned to read and enjoy poetry, there's no time like the present. It's there to serve you. Poetry, like music, improves with use. Familiarize yourself with the poem prescription by reading it over and over—preferably aloud. Wring out of it all you can get. Make it an indelible image on your brain. Say the sound of it repeatedly, until you can recall at least parts of it at different times during the day. It's very important to read the poem out loud. Poetry is sound and rhythm as well as message, and there's something very beneficial in hearing your own voice recite the poem—as though by saying it you are reaffirming what it says.

Why does poetry work to relieve human emotion and crisis? The poet is the interpreter of emotion. He was bent on his search long before the world ever heard of Sigmund Freud. Freud himself recognized this. "Poets," he said, "were the first to salvage from the whirlpool of their emotions the deepest truths to which we others have to force our way, ceaselessly groping among torturing uncertainties."

Dr. Henry Brill, psychiatrist and director of Pilgrim State Hospital, wrote me, "We are witnessing a renaissance. Poetry therapy was well described in ancient Greek literature. It still appears to retain its value for purging the soul and cleansing the mind."

The poet himself—seeking and searching for the explanation of mysteries, and hoping, through the far reaches of his own mind and thought, to untangle some of the doubts, worries, and intricacies of living—knew his way was a healing way. "The Day Is Done" by Henry Wadsworth Longfellow tells this simply.

The day is done, and the darkness
Falls from the wings of night,
As a feather is wafted downward
From an eagle in his flight.

I see the lights of the village
Gleam through the rain and the mist,
And a feeling of sadness comes o'er me
That my soul cannot resist.

A feeling of sadness and longing,
That is not akin to pain,
And resembles sorrow only
As the mist resembles rain.

Come, read to me some poem,
Some simple and heartfelt lay,
That shall soothe this restless feeling,
And banish the thoughts of day.

Not from the grand old masters,
Not from the bards sublime,
Whose distant footsteps echo
Through the corridors of time.

For, like strains of martial music,
Their mighty thoughts suggest
Life's endless toil and endeavor,
And tonight I long for rest.

Read from some humbler poet,
Whose songs gushed from his heart,
As showers from the clouds of summer,
Or tears from the eyelids start.

Who, through long days of labor,
And nights devoid of ease,
Still heard in his soul the music
Of wonderful melodies.

Such songs have power to quiet
The restless pulse of care,
And come like the benediction
That follows after prayer.

Then read from the treasured volume
The poem of thy choice,
And lend to the rhyme of the poet
The beauty of thy voice.

And the night shall be filled with music
And the cares that infest the day
Shall fold their tents like the Arabs,
And as silently, steal away.

Poetry meets all moods and conditions. Sometimes it's pleasant to feel sad. If, like Longfellow, your mood is mellow and sad, it won't hurt to indulge it with poetry briefly. But, when you've had it with the mood of soft rain and gentle sadness, try a prescription from "Pippa Passes" by Robert Browning to reverse your feelings.

The year's at the spring
The day's at the morn:
Morning's at seven;
The hillside's dew-pearled;
The lark's on the wing;
The snail's on the thorn;
God's in His heaven—
All's right with the world!

And finally, write your own poetry, but not with an eye to publication or in fear of criticism. Write what's in you—but try to conform somewhat to rhythm and meter, because without them what you write is apt to be prose and not poetry.

Sally and Carter Craigie are poetry therapists working as a husband-wife team with mentally ill children in Philadelphia. They pull fantastic amounts of poetry from those children. The first group of poems they wrote were mimeographed and put together as a homemade book, which they titled *Feelings*. The second collection was called *More Feelings,* and finally a third volume appeared titled *Still More Feelings.* The youngsters write copiously. Most of what they write shows a developing insight and a change from destructive feelings to something brighter and more positive.

Linda, at sixteen, has attempted suicide so often she is permanently scarred and damaged. She walks with a limp that resulted from jumping from a fourth-story window, and has livid scars on her arms from razors and knives. After being with the therapy group for a while, she showed me a poem she'd written: "I feel like a flower / That has been closed up a long time / Too long / By the frost / And is now about to unfold."

Poetry

by Alison Wyrley Birch

Poetry does not complicate the arrangement of words.
It's a simplifying process instead.
A sculptor takes clay and pushes it around until it becomes
What his instinct tells him is the result that his eyes want to see.
Poetry is word-sculpture; the material of sentence shape and form
Are the armature, the clay, the bronze.
Poetry is music in another form; it's prose with a melody.
It serves the deepest need to communicate. It's imperative, it's
desperate,
It's hardly ever sweet and light.
It has honesty, but its soul is ambiguity.
It demands co-operation of the reader.
Why poetry? Why anything?
Out of all art comes understanding. Even the poet who gropes
for expression
And fails, contributes to the torrent of sounds in the universe
That need release and a listening ear.
The audience is a poem's birth.
If I threw a tennis ball against the side of a barn
All I would get back would be my tennis ball.
If I put a poem out, it dies if it isn't heard.
I don't want my poem back; it already happened to me.
If I could speak in five languages, my expression would reach
Only a fraction of its potential listeners.

I'd have to be heard in five languages, too.
I say, "Today the rain came down." It's well enough said.
A poet can make that sentence sing; can bring back one hundred
rainy nights,

Can cool your head and warm your feet,
Can make the rain sing or howl in your ear.
It can whisper of a million memories of tenderness,
Pain, cold, helplessness and fear.
Any required emotion is in the rain;
The poet finds it and gives it to you and you keep the part you
want.

I know when I read a poem, it has something to do with me.
If I smile, it's a poem; if I laugh, if I'm shocked, stabbed or hurt.
If I'm reminded of something, it's a poem.
Poetry has to be felt and heard; it must be absorbed and touched.
If it touches you back—the poem is yours.

I
Depression

Depression, the psychiatric experts say, is hidden anger. Whatever its source, it hits all of us at one time or another. There are days when it seems that nothing can go right and whatever you try to do, you know you're going to muff it. Yet most of us will admit that even in the depths of discouragement with ourselves and the world there are still some bright aspects—if we want to find them. Indulging in discouragment can be mildly pleasant too, like indulging in sadness. If we've formed a poor self-image, there can be some element of success in living up to it. We knew we were no good! Sometimes, the hidden anger is turned inward. It's comforting to know that the great William Shakespeare felt the same way.

> When, in disgrace with fortune and men's eyes,
> I all alone beweep my outcast state
> And trouble deaf heaven with my bootless cries
> And look upon myself and curse my fate,
> Wishing me like to one more rich in hope,
> Featured like him, like him with friends possess'd,
> Desiring this man's art and that man's scope,
> With what I most enjoy contented least;
> Yet in these thoughts myself almost despising,
> Haply I think on thee, and then my state,
> Like to the lark at break of day arising
> From sullen earth, sings hymns at heaven's gate;
> For thy sweet love remember'd such wealth brings
> That then I scorn to change my state with kings.

If Shakespeare, who has worn his unique crown as the greatest poet in the English language for almost four hundred years, could sink now and again to the depths of depression and self-hatred, then it's all right if we do too.

Depression requires a long look at the facts of existence, many of which can best be found in nature. Poetry brings you close to nature by plucking forth one aspect of it and relating it to the human experience.

I remember a day with a friend of mine on Fisher's Island in Long Island Sound. We'd flown in her small, four-place Cessna from the northwest corner of Connecticut diagonally across the state to the southeast corner. It was Nancy Tier's forty-third year as an aviatrix. During that time, she'd served with the Civil Air Patrol as a full colonel in World War II and had flown into every one of the forty-eight continental United States for the fun of it. We'd landed on Fisher's Island and were walking about, beachcombing and talking. "Look!" she said to me, suddenly. "There's a mockingbird." We watched as the little fellow fell from a limb onto the air in a great and obvious ecstasy, and soared on a wave of wind toward the sky. "I love a mockingbird," Nancy said then. "They fly for the pure, wild joy of it." Her identification with the bird was so complete and intense that it made the moment one of great emotion, and she spoke poetically.

A doctor once told me, "In moments of great stress, people speak pure poetry." Then he spoke about the mother of one of his patients, whom he had just told that her unmarried eighteen-year-old daughter was pregnant. "She was wonderful," he said. "She put her arms around the youngster, who was crying, and said, 'Honey, in the whole great stream of history, this little moment is only a bubble.'"

The poet brings man and nature together and leaves us with a deeper understanding of the human condition. He helps us to understand our own animal origins, and intensifies our relationship to the earth and things of it. To touch a poem is like touching home base. As soon as we re-establish ourselves in the earthly universe by way of a poem, distortions fall into more symmetrical, realistic, and pleasant patterns. Walt Whitman, who was a poet of the people, knew where to go to get his bearings again—to the animals. When we go there with him, we return renewed.

I think I could turn and live with the animals, they are so placid
                                        and self-contained;
I stand and look at them long and long.
They do not sweat and whine about their condition;
They do not lie awake in the dark and weep for their sins;
They do not make me sick discussing their duty to God;
Not one is dissatisfied—not one is demented with the mania of
                                        owning things;
Not one kneels to another, nor to his kind that lived thousands of
                                        years ago;
Not one is responsible or industrious over the whole earth.

The opposite of depression is, of course, unreserved joy and self-satisfaction, and the best antidote for the pain of depression is a prescription for pure joy. The greatest delight is in the magnitude and magnificence of everyday things. A poem that is unsurpassed in its joy in the commonplace is Emily Dickinson's poem about a train—a means of travel that her own father had worked to bring to her home town of Amherst, Massachusetts.

> I like to see it lap the miles,
> And lick the valleys up,
> And stop to feed itself at tanks;
> And then, prodigious, step
>
> Around a pile of mountains,
> And, supercilious, peer
> In shanties by the sides of roads;
> And then a quarry pare
>
> To fit its sides, and crawl between,
> Complaining all the while
> In horrid, hooting stanza;
> Then chase itself down hill
>
> And neigh like Boanerges;
> Then, punctual as a star,
> Stop—docile and omnipotent—
> At its own stable door.

It's hard to maintain a depressed state, brooding randomly about one's magnificent shortcomings, in the face of such unstilted pleasure in a rumbling, loud, outrageous iron beast. "Travel" by Edna St. Vincent Millay is another poem of joy in living and being.

> The railroad track is miles away,
> And the day is loud with voices speaking,
> But there isn't a train goes by all day
> But I hear its whistle shrieking.
>
> All night there isn't a train goes by,
> Though the night is still for sleep and dreaming
> But I see its cinders red on the sky,
> And hear its engine steaming.
>
> My heart is warm with the friends I make,
> And better friends I'll not be knowing;
> Yet there isn't a train I wouldn't take,
> No matter where it's going.

If the depression is genuine and you've really goofed it up, as we all do now and then, there's a poetic prescription for you in Edwin Markham's "Victory in Defeat."

> Defeat may serve as well as victory
> To shake the soul and let the glory out.
> When the great oak is straining in the wind,
> The boughs drink in a new beauty, and the trunk
> Sends down a deeper root on the windward side.
> Only the soul that knows the mighty grief
> Can know the mighty rapture. Sorrows come
> To stretch our spaces in the heart for joy.

The healing job of the poet is also to show, irresistibly, how close hope always is to despair. Much of the healing power in poetry is here, particularly when the poet's mood matches your own and you follow him out of his alley of doubt and gloom. Thomas Hardy has a good example of this in his "The Darkling Thrush." Try this prescription on a dark day.

I leant upon a coppice gate
When Frost was specter-gray,
And Winter's dregs made desolate
The weakening eye of day.
The tangled bine-stems scored the sky
Like strings of broken lyres,
And all mankind that haunted nigh
Had sought their household fires.

The land's sharp features seemed to be
The Century's corpse outleant,
His crypt the cloudy canopy,
The wind his death lament.
The ancient pulse of germ and birth
Was shrunken hard and dry,
And every spirit upon earth
Seemed fervorless as I.

At once a voice arose among
The bleak twigs overhead
In a full-hearted evensong
Of joy illimited;
An aged thrush, frail, gaunt and small,
In blast-beruffled plume,
Had chosen thus to fling his soul
Upon the growing gloom.

So little cause for carolings
Of such ecstatic sound
Was written on terrestrial things
Afar or night around,
That I could think there trembled through
His happy good-night air
Some blessed hope, whereof he knew
But I was unaware.

    "Great Things" is another Hardy poem that makes something
rapturous and romantic out of the elements of life to which most of
us have access.

Sweet cyder is a great thing,
A great thing to me.
Spinning down to Weymouth town
Or Ridgeway thirstily.

And maid and mistress summoning
Who tend the hostelry:
O cyder is a great thing,
A great thing to me.

The dance it is a great thing,
A great thing to me,
With candles lit and partners fit
For night-long revelry.

And going home when day-dawning
Peeps pale upon the lea:
O dancing is a great thing,
A great thing to me.

Love is, yea, a great thing,
A great thing to me,
When having drawn across the lawn
In darkness silently,

A figure flits like one a-wing
Out from the nearest tree:
O love is, yea, a great thing,
A great thing to me.

Will these be always great things,
Great things to me?
Let it befall that One will call,
"Soul, I have need of thee."

What then? Joy jaunts, impassioned flings
Love and its ecstasy,
Will always have been great things,
Great things to me.

Contentment is also opposed to depression, if not quite so diametrically as joy. Perhaps the spirit more often seeks a calm solace

than unmitigated bliss. If you don't want to be lifted out of your pain on the waves of wild happiness but do want some little better measure of peace than possesses you now, try a prescription of William Butler Yeats' "The Lake Isle Of Innisfree":

I will arise and go now, and go to Innisfree,
And a small cabin built there, of clay and wattles made;
Nine bean rows will I have there, a hive for the honey bee
And live alone in the bee-loud glade.

And I shall have some peace there, for peace comes dropping
slow,
Dropping from the veils of the morning to where the cricket
sings.

There's midnights all a-glimmer, and noon a purple glow
And evenings full of linnet's wings.

I will arise and go now, for always, night and day
I hear lake water lapping, with low sounds by the shore!
While I stand on the roadway, or on the pavements gray,
I hear it in the deep heart's core.

To all of us there are moments of nostalgia and memory that hold sadness in. We mourn that times have changed, friends have moved. There are the semisweet, semisad recollections of past pleasure or joy. At times like these our depressions are only a little painful. A rainy night, a fire on the hearth, and a few wraiths of the past stir beside us. We don't really want the mood to go; we want it heightened and sustained. We want something out of the moment that will make it more than maudlin, something to give it character and value and life. If it is an old love that haunts you, try taking one sonnet of Edna St. Vincent Millay's:

Time does not bring relief; you all have lied
Who told me time would heal me of my pain!
I miss him in the weeping of the rain;
I want him in the shrinking of the tide;
The old snows melt from every mountain side,
And last year's leaves are smoke in every lane;
But last year's bitter loving must remain

Heaped on my heart and my old thoughts abide,
There are a hundred places where I fear
To go—so with his memory they brim.
And entering with relief some quiet place
Where never fell his foot or shone his face
I say "There is no memory of him here!"
And so stand stricken, so remembering him.

and mix it with another of her poems, "Song of Second April."

April this year, not otherwise
Than April of a year ago,
Is full of whispers, full of sighs,
Of dazzling mud and dingy snow;
Hepaticas that pleased you so
Are here again, and butterflies.

There rings a hammering all day
And shingles lie about the doors;
In orchards near and far away
The grey woodpecker taps and bores;
And men are merry at their chores,
And children earnest at their play.

The larger streams run still and deep,
Noisy and swift the small brooks run;
Among the mullein stalks the sheep
Go up the hillside in the sun,
Pensively—only you are gone,
You that alone I cared to keep.

If not an old love, maybe it's an old place you long for—an old
home perhaps, or somewhere where you were once particularly
happy. Doctors fight poison with poison sometimes, and fire-fighters
fight fire with fire. Fight the mood of nostalgia and remembrance
with a poem of the same mood. Again, Edna St. Vincent Millay,
"Exiled."

Searching my heart for its true sorrow,
This is the thing I find to be:

Poetry for Peace of Mind

That I am weary of words and people,
Sick of the city, wanting the sea.

Wanting the sticky, salty sweetness
Of the strong wind and shattered spray;
Wanting the loud sound and the soft sound
Of the big surf that breaks all day.

Always before about my dooryard,
Marking the reach of the winter sea,
Rooted in sand and dragging driftwood,
Struggled the purple wild sweet-pea.

Always I climbed the wave at morning,
Shook the sand from my shoes at night,
That now am caught beneath great buildings,
Stricken with noise, confused with light.

If I could hear the green piles groaning
Under the windy wooden piers,
See once again the bobbing barrels,
And the black sticks that fence the weirs.

If I could see the weedy mussels
Crusting the wrecked and rotting hulls,
Hear once again the hungry crying
Overhead of the wheeling gulls,

Feel once again the shanty straining
Under the turning of the tide,
Fear once again the rising freshet,
Dread the bell in the fog outside,

I should be happy! That was happy
All day long on the coast of Maine;
I have a need to hold and handle
Shells and anchors and ships again!

I should be happy that am happy
Never at all since I came here.
I am too long away from water
I have a need of water near.

Soon, the sustained sadness will have to go; only a small amount of it can serve you; otherwise you will sink into a full-scaled depression. Quickly now! Try John Masefield's "Laugh and Be Merry." It's a great prescription to be taken with the last of the nostalgia poems.

Laugh and be merry, remember, better the world with a song,
Better the world with a blow in the teeth of a wrong.
Laugh for the time is brief, a thread the length of a span.
Laugh and be proud to belong to the old proud pageant of man.

Laugh and be merry: remember, in olden time
God made Heaven and Earth for joy he took in a rime,
Made them, and filled them full with the strong red wine of His
                                                              mirth,
The splendid joy of the stars: the joy of the earth.

So we must laugh and drink from the deep blue cup of the sky,
Join the jubilant song of the great stars sweeping by,
Laugh, and battle, and work, and drink of the wine outpoured
In the dear green earth, the sign of the joy of the Lord.

Laugh and be merry together, like brothers akin,
Guesting awhile in the rooms of a beautiful inn.
Glad till the dancing stops, and the lilt of the music ends.
Laugh till the game is played; and be you merry, my friends.

This collection of poems to combat depression has taken you through from discouragement and self-hatred to nostalgic sadness and joy. Now, here's one last prescription for depression from the great poet John Milton. Some of his depression was justified by his very real blindness, but even then he could wing out of it on the back of a poem. Here is "On His Blindness."

> When I consider how my light is spent
> Ere half my days in this dark world and wide,
> And that one talent which is death to hide
> Lodged with me useless, though my soul more bent
> To serve therewith my Maker and present
> My true account, lest He returning chide:
> "Doth God exact day labor, light denied?"
> I fondly ask. But Patience, to prevent
> That murmur, soon replies, "God doth not need
> Either man's work or his own gifts; who best
> Bear his mild yoke, they serve him best; his state
> Is kingly; thousands at his bidding speed,
> And post o'er land and ocean without rest;
> They also serve who only stand and wait."

II
Guilt

Something in the way parents rear their children often fosters built-in guilt in the later adult. The right and wrong of things is brought home so indelibly that all our later life is spent in a series of rounds with guilt. Some have it to a lesser degree than others, but it seems no one is totally free. In the shadows of our daily existence guilt stalks secretly, appearing at the least expected moment to make us distraught about our work; or because we don't feel what we consider is the right amount of love for our parents, our children, or our neighbors; or because we are inwardly angry. And lately we've taken on the guilts of the universe in our attitudes toward our country and ourselves.

Robert Frost knew and understood why a conscientious factory worker could just not care one day if he missed the starting whistle. In his "Lone Striker" you feel the protagonist come to grips with his guilt about his work and his responsibilities. The "Lone Striker" is the best prescription for guilty feelings about goofing off that you can take.

> The swinging mill bell changed its rate
> To tolling like the count of fate.
> And though at that the tardy ran,
> One failed to make the closing gate.
> There was a law of God or man
> That on the one who came too late
> The gate for half an hour be locked,
> His time be lost, his pittance docked.

He stood rebuked and unemployed.
The straining mill began to shake.
The mill, though many, many eyed,
Had eyes inscrutably opaque;
So that he couldn't look inside
To see if some forlorn machine
Was standing idle for his sake.
(He couldn't hope its heart would break.)

And yet he thought he saw the scene:
The air was full of dust of wool.
A thousand yarns were under pull,
But pull so slow, with such a twist.
All day from spool to lesser spool,
It seldom overtaxed their strength;
They safely grew in slender length.
And if one broke by any chance,
The spinner saw it at a glance.
The spinner still was there to spin.

That's where the human still came in.
Her deft hand showed with finger rings
Among the harp-like spread of strings.
She caught the pieces end to end
And with a touch that never missed,
Not so much tied as made them blend.
Man's ingenuity was good.
He saw it plainly where he stood,
Yet found it easy to resist.

He knew another place, a wood,
And in it, tall as trees, were cliffs;
And if he stood on one of these,
'Twould be among the tops of trees,
Their upper branches round him wreathing,
Their breathing mingled with his breathing.
If—if he stood! Enough of ifs!
He knew a path that wanted walking;
He knew a spring that wanted drinking;
A thought that wanted further thinking;
A love that wanted re-newing.

Poetry for Peace of Mind

Nor was this just a way of talking
To save him the expense of doing.
With him it boded action, deed.

The factory was very fine;
He wished it all the modern speed.
Yet, after all, 'twas not divine,
That is to say 'twas not a church.
He never would assume that he'd
Be any institution's need.
But he said then, and still would say
If there should ever come a day
When industry seemed like to die
Because he left it in the lurch,
Or even merely seemed to pine
For want of his approval, why,
Come get him—they knew where to search.

If the "Lone Striker" isn't enough and guilt still possesses you for
supposed laziness, or the urge just to throw in the towel, you can
mix this poem with it. You can't overdose; a little of W. H. Davies'
"Leisure" will only be beneficial.

What is this life, if, full of care,
We have no time to stand and stare.

No time to stand beneath the boughs
And stare as long as sheep or cows.

No time to see when woods we pass,
Where squirrels hide their nuts in grass.

No time to see, in broad daylight,
Streams full of stars, like skies at night.

No time to turn at beauty's glance,
And watch her feet, how they can dance.

No time to wait till her mouth can
Enrich that smile her eyes began.

A poor life this, if, full of care,
We have no time to stand and stare.

One of my poems, called "Pacific Dawn," is a prescription for the work-guilt syndrome:

A silver carpeting of sand
Slipped silently forward toward the sea
Spreads sheer and neat from where I stand
To where the morning's going to be.
Cool silver and grey silence lies
On everything—the trees draw straight
And hold their silence for the rise
Of dawn, and all things wait.
Slight specks of pink against the grey,
The lesser tinge—the sea rolls in
Throwing its great salt waves away
At where the last, late tide had been.
The sandpiper on sticklike legs
Runs swiftly as the surf recedes
To where the very last salt dregs
Clings to the sand—transparent beads.
Then as the mighty waves gain force,
Inhaling weeds and beads and sand
And spewing it out upon the course
It's bent on following to land,
The tiny sand bird runs pursued
Back to the body of the shore,
As if the angry surf had shooed
The little fellow from its door,
Then suddenly, dawn breaks the sky
In passionate and livid light.
The white clouds, bruised and purple, try
To scurry safely out of sight
To race the duty and demand
Of industry—the little bird
Still runs upon the sand.

"Wanderlust" is also mine:

It's a strange, wild force
That the wanderer knows

To travel over the sea and air,
And lay back the land
Till the marrow shows
From the bones of the centuries buried there.
It's a taunting tune
That the wind allows,
And a tuft of cloud makes the sky seem strong.
Earth is renouncing
All its vows
To hurry the vagabond along.
It's a pensive force
That is green and new
That makes the wanderer wish his dream.
To the old it is youth
That is pushing through.
To the young, it's the oak leaf on the stream.

Because it's such a common feeling, here's a final work-guilt prescription from Robert Frost—his famous "Stopping by Woods on a Snowy Evening."

Whose woods these are I think I know.
His house is in the village though;
He will not see me stopping here
To watch his woods fill up with snow.

My little horse must think it queer
To stop without a farmhouse near
Between the woods and frozen lake
The darkest evening of the year.

He gives his harness bells a shake
To ask if there is some mistake.
The only other sound's the sweep
Of easy wind and downy flake.

The woods are lovely, dark and deep.
But I have promises to keep,
And miles to go before I sleep,
And miles to go before I sleep.

You don't need to search far for a prescription for the guilt we all seem to bear today against war and world conditions. We are not a violent people and we have progressed far from the depths of great violence in the past into something that is now nearing genuine civilization. All that is needed as a prescription for peace in this quarter is a look at history. I wrote a little poem about this myself, which appeared in the *Wall Street Journal's* "Salt and Pepper" column.

> Every day when I pursue
> Any media for news,
> Hopes that once were high now fail
> And thoughts of suicide prevail.
>
> Then I will go and take a look
> In some ancient history book,
> And hope returns for, more or less,
> The world has always been a mess.

History will remind you of the antidraft rioting in which thousands were killed in New York during the Civil War. It will remind you of the massacres of Indians in which whole villages were "self-righteously" wiped out. It will recall for you the religious inquisitions, the massacre of the Huguenots on St. Bartholemew's Eve, the tossing of live Christians to the lions in the good old days of Rome. Thomas Hardy has a prescription for the easement of guilt feelings about modern war in his "Channel Firing."

> That night your great guns, unawares,
> Shook all our coffins as we lay,
> And broke the chancel window-squares,
> We thought it was the Judgment-day
>
> And sat upright. While drearisome
> Across the howl of wakened hounds.
> The mouse let fall the altar-crumb,
> The worms drew back into the mounds,
>
> The glebe cow drooled. Till God called, "No;
> It's gunnery practice out at sea

Just as before you went below;
The world is as it used to be:

All nations striving hard to make
Red war yet redder. Mad as hatters
They do no more for Christes sake
Than you who are helpless in such matters.

That this is not the judgment-hour
For some of them's a blessed thing,
For if it were they'd have to scour
Hell's floor for so much threatening . . .

Ha, ha, It will be warmer when
I blow the trumpet (if indeed
I ever do; for you are men,
And rest eternal sorely need.)"

So down we lay again. "I wonder
Will the world ever saner be,"
Said one, "than when He sent us under
In our indifferent century!"

And many a skeleton shook his head.
"Instead of preaching forty year,"
My neighbor, Parson Thirdly, said,
"I wish I'd stuck to pipes and beer."

Again the guns disturbed the hour,
Roaring their readiness to avenge,
As far inland as Stourton Tower,
And Camelot, and starlit Stonehenge.

One of the most guilt-ridden situations in life centers around the relationships of parents and children. On both sides, there is constant internal questioning. Is our behavior real? Are our feelings right? Have we done enough, or too much, for our parents or our children? Where does love and duty begin? Just what is our duty? The first prescription for these doubts comes from *The Prophet* by Kahlil Gibran.

And a woman who held a babe against
Her bosom said, "Speak to us of children"

And he said:
"Your children are not your children.
They are the sons and daughters of Life's
Longing for itself.
They come through you but not from you,
And though they are with you, yet they
Belong not to you.

You may give them your love but not
Your thoughts,
For they have their own thoughts.
You may house their bodies but not
Their souls,
For their souls dwell in the house of to-morrow,
Which you cannot visit, not even in your dreams.
You may strive to be like them, but seek
Not to make them like you.
For life goes not backwards nor tarries
With yesterday.

You are the bows from which your children
As living arrows are sent forth.
The archer sees the mark upon the path
Of the infinite, and he bends you with his might
That his arrows may go swift and far.
Let your bending in the archer's hand
Be for gladness!
For even as he loves the arrow that flies,
So he loves also the bow that is stable."

E. E. Cummings' poem "Anyone Lived in a Pretty How Town"
is an epic of averageness in the intense and simple joys and
sorrows of life between a man, his wife, and his children. If you
read it a few times, the rhythm will get to you; you'll begin to see
the shape of family existence. You'll see that no matter what anyone
does or doesn't do for anyone else, life for each of us goes pretty
much on its own strange but average course. Moons rise and set;
suns grow round and disappear; children grow up and they forget
and remember; and still, anyone's life is a dance of joy one moment
and protracted pain the next. Sleeping, waking, dreaming—Cum-

Poetry for Peace of Mind

mings' "anyone" is fortunate to have his life partner (no one) unalterably devoted to him throughout the strange rhythmic dance of existence.

> anyone lived in a pretty how town
> (with up so floating many bells down)
> spring, summer, autumn, winter
> he sang his didn't he danced his did.
>
> women and men (both little and small)
> cared for anyone not at all
> they sowed their isn't they reaped their same
> sun, moon, stars, rain
>
> children guessed (but only a few
> and down they forgot as up they grew)
> autumn, winter, spring, summer
> that no one loved him more by more.

when by now and tree by leaf
she laughed his joy and she cried his grief
bird by snow and stir by still
anyone's any was all to her

someones married their everyones
laughed their cryings and did their dance
(sleep, wake, hope and then) they
said their nevers they slept their dreams

stars, rain, sun, moon
(and only the snow can begin to explain
how children are apt to forget to remember
with up so floating many bells down)

one day anyone died i guess
(and no one stooped to kiss his face)
busy folks buried them side by side
little by little and was by was

all by all and deep by deep
and more by more they dream their sleep
no one and anyone earth by april
wish by spirit and if by yes

women and men (both dong and ding)
summer, autumn, winter, spring
reaped their sowing and went their came
sun, moon, stars, rain

Guilt, like depression, isn't always traceable. Sometimes it attacks us without a foundation. We just feel wrong, without any tangible wrongdoing to hang our symptoms on. Stephen Crane has a poem prescription for this kind of weird malady in "It Was Wrong to Do This Said the Angel."

"It was wrong to do this," said the angel.
"You should live like a flower,
  Holding Malice like a puppy,
  Waging war like a lambkin."

Poetry for Peace of Mind

"Not so" quoth the man
  Who had no fear of spirits:
"It is only wrong for angels
  Who can live like flowers,
    Holding malice like the puppies,
    Waging war like the lambkins."

You might take Crane a few times daily, mixed with A. E. Housman's "Others, I Am Not the First."

Others, I am not the first,
Have willed more mischief than they durst:
If in the breathless night I too
Shiver now, 'tis nothing new.

More than I, if truth were told,
Have stood and sweated hot and cold,
And through their veins in ice and fire
Fear contented with desire.

Agued once like me were they,
But I like them shall win my way
Lastly to the bed of mould
Where there's neither heat nor cold.

But from my grave across my brow
Plays no wind of healing now,
And fire and ice within me fight
Beneath the suffocating night.

And add Theodore Roethke's "The Waking Just Before Sleeping."

I wake to sleep and take my waking slow.
I feel my fate in what I cannot fear.
I learn by going where I have to go.

We think by feeling. What is there to know?
I hear my being dance from ear to ear.
I wake to sleep and take my waking slow.

Of those so close beside me, which are you
God bless the ground! I shall walk softly there.
And learn by going where I have to go.

Light takes the tree, but who can tell us how?
The lowly worm climbs up a winding stair;
I wake to sleep, and take my waking slow.

The myth called success has been bashed into our heads by our culture, our parents, our society—that strange group of misfits who always know best what others should be doing. From kindergarten up, strangers have told us that we ought to be out there, leading. Our parents made much of our first miserable little successes, like our first drawings, our first written words; but always over our heads hung the Sword of Greater Happenings. Every mother's son was to be president. Every daughter was to marry a prince. It placed a lifetime of hardship on most of us who simply couldn't make it. Most of us grow up doing well at the work we either selected or have had thrust upon us. Still, there's that nagging little bit of discomfort that creeps up now and again, when we feel that somewhere along the way we got off the trolley at the wrong stop. Then it's time to remember that even those who count great successes on their side of the scale today will be forgotten in the mist of history. There's only one Shakespeare, one Abe Lincoln. Posterity will have to do without the great works of the masses of us who live decent, hardworking, and sometimes happy lives, but who haven't got the torch in our hands to carry our flame and fame down through history.

When it bothers you a little, try Emily Dickinson. Here was a genius who lived in self-imposed seclusion as a recluse in her father's Massachusetts mansion, turning out brilliant, half-cut, many-faceted diamonds of poetry and wrapping them in bundles that she hid in her bureau drawers. "Success?" she said. "Who needs it!"

Success is counted sweetest
By those who ne'er succeed.
To comprehend a nectar
Requires sorest need.

Poetry for Peace of Mind

Not one of all the purple host
Who took the flag today
Can tell the definition,
So clear, of victory.

As he, defeated, dying,
On whose forbidden ear
The distant strains of triumph
Break agonized and clear.

Morris R. Morrison, a college English teacher who has done a lot with poetry in dealing with disturbed adolescents, tells, in Dr. Jack Leedy's book *Poetry Therapy*, of Lorene. At sixteen Lorene was almost completely withdrawn. Her long hair covered her face and she kept her head averted, scratching miserably at eczema that she refused to have treated. She was on home study because she would not go to classes. Lorene never left her home. Her mother worked as a domestic and was gone most of the day. Nothing seemed to draw Lorene out of herself, although she worked fairly diligently at her studies. In the pursuit of English literature, teacher and student came across Emily Dickinson's poem "I'm Nobody! Who Are You?"

I'm nobody! Who are you?
Are you nobody too?
Then there's a pair of us!
Don't tell! They'd banish us you know!
How dreary to be somebody!
How public—like a frog—
To tell your name the livelong June
To an admiring bog!

"Something remarkable followed," Morrison said. "Lorene asked me for information. She wanted to learn something about the poet's life. I told her the story of Emily Dickinson; of her idiosyncrasies, her isolation, her unhappiness, of the posthumous discovery of her poems and her brilliant position today in world literature. She was fascinated."

Not long after this, Lorene brushed her hair away from her face and began going for treatments for her skin. Then to church. That fall she returned to her regular classes in high school. As Morrison said, "The line, 'I'm nobody,' must have moved her strongly, reflecting as it probably did, her own opinion of herself. . . . After this discovery of kinship with a celebrated writer, she could accept her own self."

Guilt is destructive. It destroys happiness in yourself and others. In almost every instance it's false guilt, a poison much more alien to your system than the nontoxic ingredients of the prescriptions for it.

III
Grief

※

Sooner or later most of us will experience grief. Grief is most often associated with loss, in any of its forms. Grief stems from a sense of hopelessness, but living almost always secretes a measure of hope. It's this measure that poetry goes to work upon. Grief can result from a loss of love. It can result from the belief in the hopelessness of a situation that is close to you. A mother I know genuinely grieved at the marriage of her daughter to a man she felt was unworthy and incapable of making her daughter happy. Grief can result from the loss of a loving pet, or from someone close and dear to you moving too far away for companionship.

But mostly grief is the result of death. Strange it is, too, that something so inevitable still causes us our most stringent pain. One can't escape from death. As unalterably as birth, it's one of the truest, most poignant, and least comprehensible of all the facts of existence. Because of its mystery, its subtle fascination, and its inevitability, most poets at one time or another have touched it.

The nineteenth-century poet Emily Dickinson was obsessed with death and immortality. "Because I Could Not Stop for Death" has been considered by many as one of the finest poems ever written. It is as close to a panacea for grief resulting from death as it is possible to get. Something about the simplicity of the statement is immeasurably comforting. Immortality and eternity are taken for granted. Death is a pleasant trip to Emily, and there is a gentle, almost loving relationship between the living one who is leaving and the coachman who leads her to eternity.

> Because I could not stop for Death
> He kindly stopped for me;
> The carriage held but just ourselves
> And Immortality
>
> We slowly drove, he knew no haste,
> And I had put away
> My labor and my leisure too,
> For his civility.
>
> We passed the school where children played
> At wrestling in a ring:
> We passed the fields of gazing grain,
> We passed the setting sun.
>
> We passed before a house that seemed
> A swelling of the ground;
> The roof was scarcely visible,
> The cornice but a mound.
>
> Since then 'tis centuries; but each
> Feels shorter than the day
> I first surmised the horses' heads
> Were toward eternity.

The acceptance of death as a fact is the first step toward learning to bear its sting when it strikes. How can one persist in fighting and flailing against the inevitable? E. E. Cummings, as a poet, may take a little more investigation and pursuing than Emily and many others, but the investment in Cummings is worth the cost. His rhythms alone are comforting, and carry with them some of the sense of his statement. While at first glance he may seem to speak in riddles, a second and third reading blend the simple obscurities right off into the background. Then his strange language becomes even more normal than normal. Caught up in his music, his message rides on it straight to a therapeutic comprehension. Do read him out loud! Try this prescription for grief—"What If a Much of a Which of a Wind."

what if a much of a which of a wind
gives the truth to summer's lie;
bloodies with dizzying leaves the sun
and yanks immortal stars awry?
Blow king to beggar and queen to seem
(blow friend to friend; blow space to time)
—when skies are hanged and oceans drowned,
the single secret will still be man

what if a keen of a lean wind flays
screaming hills with sleet and snow:
strangles galleys by ropes of thing
and stifles forests in white ago?
Blow hope to terror; blow seeing to blind
(blow pity to envy and soul to mind)
—whose hearts are mountains, roots are trees,
it's they shall cry hello to the spring

what if dawn of a doom of a dream
bites this universe in two,
peels forever out of his grave
and sprinkles nowhere with me and you?
Blow soon to never and never to twice
(blow life to isn't: blow death to was)
—all nothing's only our hugest home;
the most who die, the more we live

One of the most powerful death poems ever written was wrung
from the bereaved poet Dylan Thomas when his father died.
It is healing in its very intensity and anger. There's a universal
comprehension to the understanding that death comes too soon to
allow man fully to explore his own potential. Yet the good night of
eternal sleep implies something beyond what we call living. Take
Thomas's "Do Not Go Gentle" as a balm for the poignancy of grief
from the loss of an elder, parent, or friend.

Do not go gentle into that good night,
Old age should burn and rave at close of day;
Rage, rage against the dying of the light.

Though wise men at their end know dark is right,
Because their words had forked no lightning they
Do not go gentle into that good night.

Good men, the last wave by, crying how bright
Their frail deeds might have danced in a green bay,
Rage, rage against the dying of the light.

Wild men who caught and sang the sun in flight,
And learn, too late, they grieved it on its way,
Do not go gentle into that good night.

Grave men, near death, who see with blinding sight
Blind eyes could blaze like meteors and be gay.
Rage, rage against the dying of the light.

And you, my father, there on the sad height
Curse, bless, me now with your fierce tears, I pray.
Do not go gentle into that good night.
Rage, rage against the dying of the light.

The following two poems on death are mine:

Death of an Average Man

He dropped the flannel sleeve
Of his grey suit.
Life was a simple seed
That struck its root

Into the damaged earth
Of his lost pride.
Youth was a foolish wish
He'd turned aside.

All that his need was here
Made others sigh.
His fingers tried to change
The patterned sky.

He fought revolving time
And changeless things

Then fought the black despair
Frustration brings.

But seeds of love were sown
Where he was blind.
And there were eyes of tears
He left behind.

Death in the Family

There was really no disturbance
On the day my father died.
A mere flutter of the eyelids
Made the death seem bona fide.

Such a violent man when living
With his temper in a rage,
It was odd to see him dying
As if turning past a page.

I had thought that he would fight it;
Have it out with death and win—
His acceptance without battle
Was not as I remember him.

I had never known him placid
Or serene, or even still.
Death took him far too easily
And much against my will.

Had he lost his life in anger,
I could let death have its way.
It was dreadful to release him
In that awful, silent way.

In spite of the painful intensities of living, life is still worth cling-
ing to. Many of the agonies of existence are, to borrow a medical
cliché, "more apparent than real." Apparent as they are, they really
don't exist except as phantoms, ghosts to scare us into believing that
life is painful, when really it's not all that bad. Somewhere along the
road from birth to maturity we got the idea that there was such a

thing as total contentment, spiced up now and again with bliss. When we fall shy of our measure, the phantoms rise and tease us in believing that life is composed of sections of pain, strung together by minor moments without it. Joy, to the average man, is no permanent household guest. Algernon Charles Swinburne has a prescription for our feeling about the whole of life:

Before the beginning of years
There came to the making of man
Time, with a gift of tears;
Grief, with a glass that ran;
Pleasure, with pain for leaven;
Summer, with flowers that fell;
Remembrance fallen from heaven,
And madness risen from hell;
Strength without hands to smite;
Love that endures for a breath;
Night, the shadow of light,
And life, the shadow of death.

And the high gods took in hand
Fire, and the falling of tears,
And a measure of sliding sand
From under the feet of the years;
And froth and drift of the sea;
And dust of the laboring earth;
And bodies of things to be
In the houses of death and of birth;
And wrought with weeping and laughter,
And fashioned with loathing and love,
With life before and after
And death beneath and above,
For a day and a night and a morrow,
That his strength might endure for a span
With travail and heavy sorrow,
The holy spirit of man.

From the winds of the north and the south
They gathered as unto strife;
They breathed upon his mouth,

They filled his body with life;
Eyesight and speech they wrought
For the veils of the soul therein.
A time for labor and thought,
A time to serve and to sin;
They gave him light in his ways,
And love and a space for delight,
And beauty and length of days,
And night, and a sleep in the night.
His speech is a burning fire;
With his lips he travaileth;
And his heart is a blind desire;
In his eyes foreknowledge of death;
He weaves and is clothed with derision;
Sows, and he shall not reap;
His life is a watch or a vision
Between a sleep and a sleep.

Theodore Roethke's "Elegy for Jane" is a prescription for remembrance of the loss of a loved one. It has a tender quality almost of joy, in spite of the true pain of bereavement.

I remember the neck curls, limp and damp as tendrils;
And her quick look, a sidelong pickerel smile;
And how, once startled into talk, the light syllables leaped for her,
And she balanced in the delight of her thought,
A wren, happy, tail into the wind,
Her song trembling the twigs and small branches.
The shade sang with her!
The leaves, their whispers turned to kissing,
And the mould sang in the bleached valleys under the rose.

Oh, when she was sad, she cast herself down in such a pure
depth,
Even a father could not find her.
Scraping her cheek against straw,
Stirring the clearest water.

My sparrow, you are not here,
Waiting like a fern, making a spiney shadow.

The sides of wet stones cannot console me,
Nor the moss, wound with the last light.

If only I could nudge you from this sleep,
My maimed darling, my skittery pigeon.
Over the damp grave I speak the words of my love;
I with no rights in this matter,
Neither father or lover.

The late Dr. Smiley Blanton, a well-known psychiatrist, used poetry in the treatment of his patients over and over again through the years of his practice. He tells of a woman whose mind was nearly deranged by the death of her eighteen-year-old son. She was able to accept the tragedy finally after she became familiar with Robert Louis Stevenson's poem "Resurgence."

He is not dead, this friend, not dead
But in the path we mortals tread
Got some few trifling steps ahead
And nearer to the end.
So that you too, once past the bend,
Shall meet again as face to face
This friend you fancy dead.
Push gaily on strong heart! The while
You travel forward mile by mile
He loiters with a backward smile
Till you can overtake.

Elizabeth Barrett Browning offers a new look at grief and a prescription for dealing with it in her poem titled simply "Grief."

I tell you, hopeless grief is passionless;
That only men incredulous of despair,
Half-taught in anguish, through the midnight air
Beat upward to God's throne in loud access
Of shrieking and reproach. Full desertness,
In souls as countries, lieth silent-bare
Under the blanching, vertical eye-glare
Of the absolute Heavens. Deep-hearted man, express

Grief for thy Dead in silence like to death—
Most like a monumental statue set
In everlasting watch and moveless woe
Till itself crumble to the dust beneath.
Touch it; the marble eyelids are not wet:
If it could weep, it could arise and go.

There's the shadow of one's own death lurking in the death of someone well-loved. Perhaps a little bit of us dies too when death takes over the living light from someone who matters much. Alfred, Lord Tennyson's "Crossing the Bar" reflects the feeling about death that many people might have. As a prescription for peace of mind in the face of grief, it's optimistic, faithful and mildly analgesic.

Sunset and evening star,
And one clear call for me!
And may there be no moaning of the bar,
When I put out to sea,

But such a tide as moving seems asleep,
Too full for sound and foam,
When that which drew from out the boundless deep
Turns again home.

Twilight and evening bell,
And after that the dark!
And may there be no sadness of farewell,
When I embark;

For though from out our bourne of Time and Place
The flood may bear me far,
I hope to see my Pilot face to face
When I have crossed the bar.

The following poem of mine was written for a very dear friend who died at the age of ninety-one, worn out with living. I called it "Death Came Too Late."

Old man—your great eyes show the simple truth
You lived too long, my dear, too long to be

Of matter any more to anyone—to you or me.
Let those dazed eyes close safely to the sky,
Let winter have its way and take your breath,
Old man there's little left for you that's good
Or new to you—don't quarrel with death.
Your portion of the universe, the bit you played
Upon the boards that time has given to you
Has run its moments of eternity
And now at last your little term is through.
Old man don't cling and hold so tight
It's over now, the drama of your days.
No one has ever had much more than this,
Just such a simple, too-extended phase.
I'll mourn for you, my dear, and I am young.
I'll let you have my tears this dying day.
Too old to matter to another one
I'll stay beside you now, my dear, I'll stay.
You lived too long, too long, old man, my dear,
There's no one left to mourn for you but I,
A stranger to you here, but I will mourn,
You outlived all who'd weep were you to die.
You're my life's destiny, and so these tears
Are genuine, and truly from my grief—
Although the last of life to you must be
An overwhelming heaven of relief.

Matthew Arnold has a prescription for the stilling of the pain of bereavement in "Requiescat."

Strew on her roses, roses,
And never a spray of yew!
In quiet she reposes;
Ah, would that I did too!

Her mirth the world required;
She bathed it in smiles of glee.
But her heart was tired, tired,
And now they let her be.

Her life was turning, turning,
In mazes of heat and sound.
But for peace her soul was yearning,
And now peace laps her round.

Her cabined, ample spirit,
It fluttered and failed for breath.
Tonight it doth inherit
The vasty hall of death.

And two by Christina Georgina Rossetti might be taken with it in a combined dose. The first is "Remember."

Remember me when I am gone away,
Gone far away into the silent land;
When you can no more hold me by the hand,
Nor I half turn to go, yet turning stay.
Remember me when no more, day by day,
You tell me our future that you planned;
Only remember me; you understand
It will be late to counsel then or pray.
Yet if you should forget me for a while
And afterwards remember, do not grieve;
For if the darkness and corruption leave
A vestige of the thoughts that once I had,
Better by far you should forget and smile
Than that you should remember and be sad.

The second is "When I Am Dead, My Dearest."

When I am dead, my dearest
Sing no sad songs for me;
Plant thou no roses at my head,
Nor shady cypress tree:
Be the green grass above me
With showers and dewdrops wet;
And if thou wilt, remember,
And if thou wilt, forget.

I shall not see the shadows,
I shall not feel the rain;
I shall not hear the nightingale
Sing on as if in pain;
And dreaming through the twilight
That doth not rise nor set,
Haply I may remember,
And haply may forget.

The futility of tears and grief is the last prescription here, for surely what has been, has been; and weeping changes things not at all. The poem is one by Lizette Woodworth Reese called "Tears."

When I consider Life and its few years—
A wisp of fog betwixt us and the sun;
A call to battle, and the battle done
Ere the last echo dies within our ears;
A rose choked in the grass; an hour of fears;
The gusts that past a darkening shore do beat;
The burst of music down an unlistening street—
I wonder at the idleness of tears.
Ye old, old dead, and ye of yesternight,
Chieftains, and bards, and keepers of the sheep,
By every cup of sorrow that you had,
Loose me from tears, and make me see aright
How each hath back what once he stayed to weep;
Homer his sight, David his little lad!

Not being alive as we know it is the normal state. Living in one body for four-score years and ten is the least space of time we have in all eternity. We were not here before we were born and we will not be here after we die, so being here is the least of our total existence. Why do we consider it so important? Why do we fear death when we have already been dead?

When the misery of bereavement struck Ardoin Casgrain during his seventies, he turned to poetry for surcease as instinctively as a physical ailment sends one scurrying to the doctor. Now, at eighty, he's wonderfully weathered widowhood and is still composing poems, finding the nearest thing to a panacea in the expression of his simple but profound verse. Here are two examples.

I Believe

I believe in laughter
For it cheers the heart.
I believe in kindness
Where we do our part.
I believe in loving
With my very soul.
I believe in working
For some worthy goal.
I believe in thinking
For the low and mean.
I believe in lifting
With some thought serene.
I believe in giving
To living all I can.
I believe in learning
To serve the plan.
I believe in living
Each and every day
So that I am giving
Kindness on the way.

One Fixed Star

To one fixed star my spirit clings,
I know that God is good.
Whatever hope on high it brings,
His love I've understood.
Whatever trials may fill my day,
Such faith doth help my fear.
Whatever hope has blessed my way,
His love is always near.

IV
Loneliness

≫

Loneliness is a strange emotion. It can drive the introverted in search of companionship even when all there is available is an unsatisfactory moment of communication—a brief encounter with the checker in a supermarket, for example. And it can drive the extroverted in. Is there, for instance, any more lonely place than a crowded bar? Or a cocktail party? A collection of desperate human beings try to make it across a void. Poetry is the lonely man's friend. In it can be found the true communication between people of like intellects. This is one of the reasons why poetry therapy is so workable with mentally ill people. They have suffered a unique and intense kind of loneliness—alienation, a total loss of communication. When the poet comes across as if on a high wire, so easily—without swaying or losing balance—it's as if he held his arms out to greet the lonely one warmly on the other side. One such poet is Ann Hoskins.

High Wire Dancers

The drums rap out our cue. We take our place
And here, outreaching over darkened space,
Stretches the nerve of wire; tight-drawn, bright . . .
A lean, incredible highway through the night
Probed by the pencil of a single light
Pointing our peril as the trumpets call

And drums command the moment . . . ours alone.
(How long, traversing vastness, have we known
There are no nets to catch us if we fall?)
No, never nets for us; the parasol
Catching the light with spangles, and the cane,
Gaudy with tinsel, serve as balance bars
To steady questing foothold and maintain
Our place between the sawdust and the stars.

The secret of exorcising the spirits of loneliness is not in a frantic
search for some human contact somewhere, but rather in a new
direction for the symptom. Robert Frost's "Good Hours" is my next
prescription for loneliness, and for following a new direction in
search of relief.

I had for my winter evening walk
No one at all with whom to talk,
But I had the cottages in a row
Up to their shining eyes in snow.

And I thought the folks within;
I had the sound of a violin;
I had a glimpse through curtain laces
Of youthful forms and youthful faces.

I had such company outward bound.
I went till there was no cottage found.
I turned and repented, but coming back
I saw no window but that was black.

Over the snow my creaking feet
Disturbed the slumbering village street
Like profanation, by your leave,
At ten o'clock of a winter eve.

The lonely poet finds company in the existence of others in his
world. He shares his silence with the sound of a violin. Coming back
through the sleeping streets it seems wrong for him to be the only
one awake, but he still shares their existence. Alone or not, bed's
probably the right place to be, and in going there he continues to
share in human existence and action.

Poetry for Peace of Mind

The next prescription follows the mood of new directions at a time of seeming abandonment. From "The Land of Heart's Desire" by William Butler Yeats:

> The wind blows out of the gates of the day,
> The wind blows over the lonely of heart,
> And the lonely of heart is withered away,
> While the fairies dance in a place apart,
> Shaking their milk-white feet in a ring,
> Tossing their milk-white arms in the air;
> For they hear the wind laugh and murmur and sing
> Of a land where even the old are fair,
> And even the wise are merry of tongue;
> But I hear a reed of Coolaney say—
> "When the wind has laughed and murmured and sung,
> The lonely of heart is withered away."

What better way to blow away loneliness and abandonment of spirit and heart than on the wind!

Why should there be a difference between aloneness and loneliness? Both are a result of a lack of people in the sense of human sharing and communicating. Aloneness is a chance to commune with the spirit and make us aware of the sweetness of solitude; or like Emily Dickinson's

> To make a prairie it takes a clover and one bee
> One clover and a bee,
> And revery.
> The revery alone will do
> If bees are few.

Loneliness is really anxiety in another form. It's a seeming certainty of abandonment or lack of love. Aloneness is when a happy husband and wife are by themselves in the house and not talking for hours, but each is content with the sense of the other in the house. Conversely, if they are together and speaking, but alienated, they can be painfully lonely.

Loneliness can drive one to go to a store or to talk to someone on the phone, but the solutions aren't there. The solutions are in turning loneliness into periods for reflection and revery, and the best route there is on the back of a poem. Loneliness requires a coming to terms with your own nature, an ingression into the id. Poetry leads you there safely, for you can share your insights with the poet. You can blame him for some of them and reach a plateau of self-evaluation with his help. When you are lonely, the last thing you need is people or even a dog or a cat. You need self-examination for self-evaluation and self-revelation. Then in the silence of the moment, you can become your own best friend.

Now, take a dose of "Alone" by Siegfried Sassoon.

> "When I am alone"—the words tripped off his tongue
>   As though to be alone was nothing strange.
> "When I was young," he said; "When I was young . . .
>   I thought of age and loneliness and change,
>   I thought how strange we grow when we're alone
>   And how unlike the selves that meet and talk
>   And blow the candles out, and say good night,
>   Alone. . . . The word is life endured and known,
>   It is the stillness where our spirits walk
>   And all but inmost faith is overthrown.

This can be mixed with a sonnet by Edna St. Vincent Millay:

> Pity me not because the light of day
> At close of day no longer walks the sky;
> Pity me not for beauties passed away
> From field and thicket as the year goes by;
> Pity me not the waning of the moon,
> Nor that the ebbing tide goes out to sea,
> Nor that a man's desire is hushed so soon,
> And you no longer look with love on me.
> This I have known always: Love is not more
> Than the wide blossom which the wind assails,
> Strewing fresh wreckage gathered in the gales;
> Pity me that the heart is slow to learn
> What the swift mind beholds at every turn.

The beauties of nature and the beauties of love ebb and flow. There is no need for pity because of the temporary cessation of love. It will either come again, or what life is inside you will prevail, and the loss of love will no longer matter.

Nature took charge of loneliness for William Wordsworth. Try his "I Wandered Lonely as a Cloud."

> I wandered lonely as a cloud
> That floats on high o'er vales and hills,
> When all at once I saw a crowd,
> A host, of golden daffodils;
> Beside the lake, beneath the trees,
> Fluttering and dancing in the breeze.
>
> Continuous as the stars that shine
> And twinkle on the milky way,
> They stretched in never-ending line
> Along the margin of a bay:
> Ten thousand saw I at a glance,
> Tossing their heads in sprightly dance.
>
> The waves beside them danced; but they
> Out-did the sparkling waves in glee:
> A poet could not but be gay
> In such a jocund company:
> I gazed—and gazed—but little thought
> What wealth the show to me had brought:
>
> For oft, when on my couch I lie
> In vacant or in pensive mood,
> They flash upon that inward eye
> Which is the bliss of solitude;
> And then my heart with pleasure fills
> And dances with the daffodils.

"Rondeau" by Leigh Hunt is a quaint and bright little poem that's helpful for dispersing the blues of loneliness. Everyone can remember a moment such as his. Read it and scan your memory for a sprightly kiss of warmth and tenderness given to you at one time or another by a child, or a friend or a genuine lover. The

"Jenny" in this poem is full nylon stretch and can fit any mold you want.

> Jenny kissed me when we met,
> Jumping from the chair she sat in;
> Time, you thief, who love to get
> Sweets into your list, put that in;
> Say I'm weary, say I'm sad,
> Say that health and wealth have missed me,
> Say I'm growing old, but add,
> Jenny kissed me.

Nature and poetry are the two great healers. Combined, they become the perfect prescription for whatever ails one. Even when a kind of wistful nostalgia prevails, poetry and nature make the soul respond to a universal rhythm. It's hard to stay angry at the world, or maintain a sense of abandonment against the fulfillment that the universe holds out to you. Try Dylan Thomas's "Poem in October" for a bout with loneliness. But read it over and over again! Each time it amounts to more, as if it grows while you read it!

> It was my thirtieth year to heaven
> Woke to my hearing from harbor and neighbor wood
> And the mussel pooled and the heron
> Priested shore
> The morning beckon
> With water praying and call of seagull and rook
> And the knock of sailing boats on the net-webbed wall
> Myself to set foot
> That second
> In the still sleeping town and set forth.
>
> My birthday began with the water-
> Birds and the birds of the winged trees flying my name
> Above the farms and the white horses
> And I rose
> In rainy autumn
> And walked abroad in a shower of all my days.
> High tide and the heron dived when I took the road

Over the border
And the gates
Of the town closed as the town awoke.

A springful of larks in a rolling
Cloud and the roadside bushes brimming with whistling
Blackbirds and the sun of October
Summery
On the hill's shoulder,
Here were fond climates and sweet singers suddenly
Come in the morning where I wandered and listened
To the rain wringing
Wind blow cold
In the wood faraway under me.

Pale rain over the dwindling harbor
And over the sea-wet church the size of a snail
With its horns through mist and the castle
Brown as owls,
But all the gardens
Of spring and summer were blooming in the tall tales
Beyond the border and under the lark-full cloud.
There could I marvel
My birthday
Away but the weather turned around.

It turned away from the blithe country
And down the other air and the blue altered sky
Streamed again a wonder of summer
With apples
Pears and currants.
But I saw in the turning so clearly a child's
Forgotten morning when he walked with his mother
Through the parables
Of sunlight
And the legends of the green chapels.

And the twice told fields of infancy
That his tears burned my cheeks and his heart moved in mine.
These were the woods the river and sea
Where a boy

In the listening
Summertime of the dead whispered the truth of his joy
To the trees and the stones and the fish in the tide.
And the mystery
Sang alive
Still in the water and singing birds.

And there I could marvel my birthday
Away but the weather turned around. And the true
Joy of the long-dead child sang burning
In the sun.
It was my thirtieth
Year to heaven stood there then in the summer noon
Though the town below lay leaved with October blood.
O may my heart's truth
Still be sung
On this high hill in a year's turning.

Some loneliness comes from the true fact of a missing person. One can be genuinely lonely for the presence of someone who, for any number of reasons, must be somewhere else. Unless the feeling of abandonment is there, the loneliness is simple and won't cause great pain. Emily Dickinson, the recluse who defied aloneness and challenged it to do its worst, produced a quaint, wistful, and nearly light prescription for dealing with loneliness from the lack of a loved one near.

> Heart! We will forget him!
> You and I—tonight!
> You may forget the warmth he gave—
> I will forget the light.
>
> When you have done, pray tell me
> That I may straight begin!
> Haste! Lest while you're lagging
> I may remember him!

Some things in nature are gregarious. Some animals herd, while others live and move alone. A stand of pines or birches may prefer each other's company, but many trees stand alone in vastness and seem not to mind the absence of a like soul. Walt Whitman recognized the loneliness as something he wouldn't wish for himself, but he couldn't help commenting on the tree's contentment.

> I saw in Louisiana a live-oak growing,
> All alone stood it, and the moss hung down from the branches!
> Without any companions it grew there, uttering joyous leaves of
>   dark green.
> And its look, rude, unbending, lusty, made me think of myself;
> But I wondered how it could utter joyous leaves, standing alone
>   there, without its friend, its lover near—for I knew I
>   could not;
> And I broke off a twig with a certain number of leaves upon it,
>   and twisted around it a little moss,
> I brought it away—and I have placed it in sight in my room,
> It is not needed to remind me of my own dear friends,
> (For I believe that I think of little else than of them)
> Yet it reminds me of a curious thing—it makes me think of manly
>   love;
> For all that, and though the live-oak glistens there in Louisiana,
>   solitary in a wide flat space,
> Uttering joyous leaves all its life, without a friend, a lover near,
> I know very well I could not.

"Revelation" by Robert Frost is a short prescription for loneliness:

> We make ourselves a place apart
> Behind light words that tease and flout,
> But oh, the agitated heart
> Till some one really finds us out.
>
> 'Tis pity if the case require
> (Or so we say) that in the end
> We speak the literal to inspire
> The understanding of a friend.
>
> But so with all, from babes that play
> At hide-and-seek to God afar,
> So all who hide too well away
> Must speak and tell us where they are.

So there you are! Speak up, and say that you hide away but really want the understanding of a friend.

Loneliness was something to contend with back in the sixteenth century, too. Through the centuries comes a prescription from Michael Drayton called "Give Me Myself." It's a reversal of a soul too tied to another to be able to breathe alone.

> You're not alone when you are still alone;
> O God! From you that I could private be!
> Since you one were, I never since was one,
> Since you in me, myself since out of me.
> Transported from myself into your being;
> Senseless with too much joy, each other seeing
> And only absent when we are together.
> Give me myself and take yourself again!
> Devise some means by how I may forsake you!
> So much is mine that doth with you remain
> That taking what is mine, with me I take you.
> You do bewitch me! O that I could fly
> From myself you, or from your own self I!

No matter how lonely you may feel at a special moment when the phone refuses to ring and everyone seems to have forgotten you, it's always possible to think of one real friend somewhere and realize you aren't really alone. Shakespeare prescribes this in one sonnet.

> When to the sessions of sweet silent thought
> I summon up remembrances of things past,
> I sigh the lack of many a thing I sought,
> And with old woes new wail my dear time's waste:
> Then can I drown an eye, unused to flow,
> For precious friends hid in death's dateless night,
> And weep afresh love's long since cancelled woe,
> And moan the expense of many a vanished sight.
> Then can I grieve at grievances forgone,
> And heavily from woe to woe tell o'er
> The sad account of fore-bemoaned moan,

> Which I new pay as if not paid before.
>> But if the while I think on thee dear friend,
>> All losses are restored and sorrows end.

Two more prescriptions for loneliness come from two widely separated women poets. In the first, Marianne Moore speaks of silence, people and the mysteries of togetherness, and the need for pauses of solitude in between.

> My father used to say,
> "Superior people never make long visits,
> Have to be shown Longfellow's grave
> Or the glass flowers at Harvard.
> Self-reliant like the cat
> That takes its prey to privacy
> The mouse's limp tail hanging like a shoelace from its mouth—

> They sometimes enjoy solitude,
> And can be robbed of speech
> By speech which has delighted them.
> The deepest feeling always shows itself in silence;
> Not in silence but restraint,"
> Nor was he insincere in saying, "Make my home your inn."
> Inns are not residences.

Edna St. Vincent Millay's "Eel Grass."

> No matter what I say,
> All that I really love
> Is the rain that flattens on the bay,
> And the eel grass in the cove,
> The jingle shells that lie and bleach
> At the tide line, and the trace
> Of higher tides along the beach;
> Nothing in this place.

And so we keep returning to the conclusion that loneliness can only be offset by establishing a relationship inside oneself with oneself; and on the outside with the things of nature, art, and poetry that make for communication in its finest form.

The last prescription is my own. I wrote it during a great bout with loneliness when my husband had to be hospitalized. Writing it helped me.

Night Visitor

There's a taste of salt in the falling rain
And loneliness rides the night again.
If the world is sad, then who am I
To watch it weep when my eyes are dry?
So comfortless I have let it wait
Outside my door in its gloomy state
And gathered my forces selfishly
To concentrate on consoling me.
I build a fire to chase the gloom
Out of my dreary living room,
And put a flame to the coffee pot—
The world may be sulking, but I am not!

Suddenly, hospitality wins
And a surreptitious sound begins.
It's the sizzle as rain and fire meet
Through the chimney flue to my warm retreat.
It was nice of the rain to come to call,
I mind the intrusion not at all.
But I've done so little to ease the pain
Of an aching world, and I can't explain
Why it should trouble itself to see
How things are going along with me.

V

Tension

Tension may be the result of anxiety or grief, or it may be nameless. Maybe it comes of itself because life buffets us about and we grow tense resisting. Whatever its cause, its effect is unpleasant. Joy, mirth, humor, and exercise all dispel tension. There's a quick effective source to go to for a fast dose of mirth and everything else that heals tension—and that's poetry. Here's the first prescription, entitled "Mirth," by Francis Beaumont, who recognized its use back in the sixteenth century.

> 'Tis mirth that fills the veins with blood,
> More than wine, or sleep, or food;
> Let each man keep his heart at ease;
> No man dies of that disease!
> He that would his body keep
> From diseases, must not weep;
> But whoever laughs and sings,
> Never he his body brings
> Into fevers, gouts or rheums,
> Or lingeringly his lungs consumes;
> Or meets with ague in his bone,
> Or catarrhs, or griping stone:
> But contented lives for aye;
> The more he laughs, the more he may!

The early centuries were as taut with confusion and tension as ours is today. I disagree with those who claim our times to be the most anxious and our problems more difficult to cope with than others in history. If it were so, then Shakespeare (lovely as his language is) would have died literarily as well as literally. But his universal images and his wisdoms apply today as well as they ever did: "The better part of valour is discretion," from *King Henry IV*, Part One—and from the same:

> If all the year were playing Holidays
> To sport would be as tedious as to work.

The truth sneaks down through the ages, and the truth is that all times are fraught with emotion and despair as well as with triumph and joy. It's a common denominator of living. William D'Avenant wrote in the mid-seventeenth century a prescription for tension that works like a ladle works when it stirs up the soup.

> Awake! Awake!
> The lark now leaves his watery nest,
> And, climbing, shakes his dewy wings,
> He takes this window for the east,
> And to implore your light he sings—
> Awake! Awake! The morn will never rise
> Till she can dress her beauty at your eyes.
>
> The merchant bows unto the seaman's star,
> The ploughman from the sun his season takes;
> But still the lover wonders what they are
> Who look for day before his mistress wakes.
> Awake! Awake! Break thro' your veils of lawn!
> Then draw your curtains, and begin the dawn!

The most distressing thing about tension is the unconscious fear that you will snap because of it. But people don't snap that readily, especially if they allow a poetic prescription to loosen the tautness they feel. William Cowper wrote a persuasive prescription in the mid-eighteenth century for the relief of tension, "Light Shining Out of Darkness."

God moves in a mysterious way
His wonders to perform;
He plants his footsteps in the sea,
And rides upon the storm.

Deep in unfathomable mines,
With never-failing skill,
He treasures up his bright designs,
And works his sovereign will.

Ye fearful saints, fresh courage take;
The clouds ye so much dread
Are big with mercy, and shall break
In blessings on your head.

Judge not the Lord by feeble sense,
But trust him for his grace;
Behind a frowning providence
He hides a smiling face.

His purposes will ripen fast,
Unfolding every hour;
The bud may have a bitter taste,
But sweet will be the flower.

Blind unbelief is sure to err,
And scan his work in vain;
God is his own interpreter,
And he will make it plain.

Writing some twenty years later, John Philpot Curran produced a prescription for tension and the blues in a poem called "Let Us Be Merry."

If sadly thinking, with spirits sinking,
Could, more than drinking, my cares compose,
A cure for sorrow from sighs I'd borrow,
And hope tomorrow would end my woes.
But as in wailing, there's naught availing,
And death unfailing will strike the blow;
Then for that reason, and for a season,
Let us be merry before we go.

To joy a stranger, a wayworn ranger,
In every danger my course I've run;
Now hope all ending, and death befriending,
His last aid lending, my cares are done.
No more a rover, or hapless lover,
My griefs are over—my glass runs low;
Then for that reason, and for a season,
Let us be merry before we go.

Tension threatens when our inner image conflicts with what we think the outer world is seeing. There is always tension when what we think we are fights with what we think we ought to be. Internal harmony comes when we recognize that we have only ourselves to answer to. All our triumphs and failures concern the world very little. They are, after all, only momentous to ourselves. We are born by ourselves, live within ourselves, and die alone, no matter who sits beside us and no matter whose hand we hold. Once this is fully realized, a great inner composure follows and we can ease up on the struggle and become friends with ourselves. Just as no single man knows every triumph we have, neither does any single man know how often we have failed. In the great stream of history, even our massive, disastrous failures are just a limpid ripple and a minor wave. Tensions melt if we can see ourselves as a person of value for our existence alone, and can cease striving for that erratic and unpredictable something called success. For a dose of inner peace, try Ralph Waldo Emerson's "The Rhodora."

In May, when sea-winds pierced our solitudes,
I found the fresh Rhodora in the woods,
Spreading its leafless blooms in a damp nook,
To please the desert and the sluggish brook.
The purple petals, fallen in the pool,
Made the black water with their beauty gay;
Here might the red-bird come his plumes to cool,
And court the flower that cheapens his array.
Rhodora! If the sages ask thee why
This charm is wasted on the earth and sky,
Tell them, Dear, that if eyes were made for seeing,
Then Beauty is its own excuse for being:

Poetry for Peace of Mind

Why thou wert there, O rival of the rose!
I never thought to ask, I never knew:
But, in my simple ignorance, suppose
The self-same Power that brought me there brought you.

If tension still possesses you, although lessened, read the poem over again aloud. Wait a few minutes for it to take effect and then add a prescription from William Wordsworth, "Upon Westminster Bridge."

Earth has not anything to show more fair:
Dull would he be of soul who could pass by
A sight so touching in its majesty:
This City now doth, like a garment, wear
The beauty of the morning; silent, bare,
Ships, towers, domes, theatres, and temples lie
Open unto the fields, and to the sky,
All bright and glittering in the smokeless air.
Never did sun more beautifully steep
In his first splendour, valley, rock, or hill;
Ne'er saw I, never felt, a calm so deep!
The river glideth at his own sweet will:
Dear God! the very houses seem asleep;
And all that mighty heart is lying still!

Tension also develops under the strain of trying to make existence meaningful in a temporal world. Death is the end of life as we know it, and whatever our faith, there is no certainty that what we are will matter beyond this restricted strata; but under the circumstances I'd say, along with some poets, that I wouldn't want to risk the nondevelopment of my soul, just in case there is another place for it to labor! That "invisible life" that makes you unique needs nourishment and development. Try Rupert Brooke's prescription for peace when fear of the hereafter produces tension and you're not sure why you're living.

If I should die, think only this of me:
That there's some corner of a foreign field
That is forever England. There shall be

In that rich earth a richer dust concealed;
A dust whom England bore, shaped, made aware,
Gave, once, her flowers to love, her ways to roam,
A body of England's, breathing English air,
Washed by the rivers, blest by suns of home.
And think, this heart, all evil shed away,
A pulse in the eternal mind, no less
Gives somewhere back the thoughts by England given;
Her sights and sounds; dreams happy as her day;
And laughter, learnt of friends; and gentleness,
In hearts at peace, under an English heaven.

A love affair with the world helps develop the soul for any future
it may have, and by doing so, dispels tension. Two prescriptions by
Thomas Hardy follow. Although sometimes sad and sorry about human relationships in his late-nineteenth- and early-twentieth-century
world, Hardy had a tender regard for all the abstracts of the universe and thereby enriched his own living.

Weathers

This is the weather the cuckoo likes,
    and so do I;
When showers betumble the chestnut spikes,
    and nestlings fly;
And the little brown nightingale bills his best,
And they sit outside at The Traveler's Rest,
And maids come forth sprig-muslin drest,
And citizens dream of the south and west,
    And so do I.

This is the weather the shepherd shuns,
    and so do I;
When beeches drip in browns and duns,
    and thresh and ply;
And hill-hid tides throb, throe on throe,
And meadow rivulets overflow,
And drops on gate-bars hang in a row,
And rooks in families homeward go,
    And so do I.

And the second prescription, "Let Me Enjoy."

> Let me enjoy the earth no less
> Because the all-enacting Might
> That fashioned forth its loveliness
> Had other aims than my delight.
>
> About my path there flits a Fair,
> Who throws me not a word or sign;
> I'll charm me with her ignoring air,
> And laud the lips not meant for mine.
>
> From manuscripts of moving song
> Inspired by scenes and sound unknown,
> I'll pour out raptures that belong
> To others as they were my own.
>
> And some day hence,
> Toward Paradise
> And all its blest—if such should be—
> I will lift glad, afar-off eyes,
> Though it contain no place for me.

Tension is physical, too. Based on an emotional beginning, it creates muscular tightness as it develops. Laughter is one of the greatest ways of reversing tension. There have been many great nonsense and limerick writers who have entertained the tensions out of readers through the years. Humor relates to the human condition, and the human condition hardly varies throughout time. Real humor is timeless. There will be more so-called "light verse" in another chapter, but for our purposes here in relieving tension, try "Jabberwocky" by Lewis Carroll.

> 'Twas brillig, and the slithy toves,
> Did gyre and gimble in the wabe;
> All mimsy were the borogoves,
> And the mome raths outgrabe.
>
> "Beware the jabberwock, my son!
> The jaws that bite, the claws that catch!
> Beware the Jubjub bird, and shun
> The frumious Bandersnatch!"

He took his vorpal sword in hand;
Long time the manxome foe he sought—
So rested he by the Tumtum tree,
And stood while in thought.

And, as in uffish thought he stood,
The Jabberwock, with eyes of flame,
Came whiffling through the tulgey wood,
And burbled as it came!

One, two! One, two! And through and through
The vorpal blade went snicker-snack!
He left it dead, and with its head
He went galumphing back.

And hast thou slain the Jabberwock?
Come to my arms, my beamish boy!
O frabjous day! Callooh, Callay!
He chortled in his joy.

'Twas brillig, and the slithy toves
Did gyre and gimble in the wabe:
All mimsy were the borogoves,
And the mome raths outgrabe.

This poem was used in a poetry therapy group with teenagers who all had emotional problems. "How does it make you feel?" the therapist asked.

"Beamish," said one boy after a moment's thought.

Internal peace is diametrically opposed to internal tension. Obviously, then, one way to rout tension is to inject peace. Coventry Patmore, writing in the nineteenth century, describes a peaceful evening scene:

The sheep-bell tolleth curfew time;
The gnats, a busy rout,
Fleck the warm air; the dismal owl
Shouteth a sleepy shout;
The voiceless bat, more felt than seen,
Is flitting round about.

The aspen leaflets scarcely stir;
The river seems to think;
Athwart, the dusk, broad primroses
Look coldly from the brink,
Where, listening to the freshet's noise,
The quiet cattle drink.

The bees boom past; the white moths rise
Like spirits from the ground;
The grey flies hum their weary tune,
A distant, dream-like sound;
And far, far off, to the slumb'rous eve,
Bayeth an old guard-hound.

As a prescription for peace of mind, try Robert Greene, sixteenth-century poet who wrote "A Mind Content."

Sweet are the thoughts that savor of content;
The quiet mind is richer than a crown;
Sweet are the nights in careless slumber spent;
The poor estate scorns fortune's angry crown:
Such sweet content, such minds, such sleep, such bliss.
Beggars enjoy, when princes oft do miss
The homely house that harbors quiet rest;
The cottage that affords no pride nor care;
The mean that 'grees with country music best;
The sweet content of mirth and music's fare;
Obscured life sets down a type of bliss:
A mind content both crown and kingdom is.

Take "A Mind Content" twice, aloud, and then add one dose of the final prescription in this group, Robert Louis Stevenson's sonnet "The Celestial Surgeon."

If I have faltered more or less
In my great task of happiness;
If I have moved among my race
And shown no glorious morning face;
If beams from happy human eyes

Have moved me not; if morning skies,
Books, and my food, and summer rain
Knocked on my sullen heart in vain—
Lord, thy most pointed pleasure take
And stab my spirit broad awake;
Or, Lord, if too obdurate I,
Choose thou, before that spirit die,
A piercing pain, a killing sin,
And to my dead heart run them in!

Whatever the dose, poetry is never toxic or lethal. There was supposed to be a sad song once that caused an increase in suicides, but the chances are pretty strong that they would have happened, with or without the song. For our purpose, it's safe to assume you can't overdose. So seek further, you seekers after relief from tension. Scan any good poetry anthology and see what takes your eye. Write poems, too. Write good ones or bad ones—just to get what is inside out, and then forget it. If you're still tense—go back to the Jabberwock and laugh again!

VI
Sleeplessness

There is a space of time after darkness lowers and before the return of light that man has set aside for sleeping. The assorted vital organs that make up the mortal work hard to keep life going, and rest is a simple requirement in return for all their effort. Closing out the world and drifting into unconsciousness is such a simple, obvious necessity, it's quite remarkable that so much of the mortal population can't seem to do it easily night after restless night.

Doctors have studied the phenomena of sleep. Our brains have been tapped and observed. Dreams have been analyzed and interpreted. Countless studies have been made to try to find an answer to sleeplessness. A million articles have been written by average citizens, each with a new trick to lure the elusive lady of the night. Drugstore shelves are filled with narcotic and nonnarcotic sleep inducers until it seems that the whole adult human world is bent only on one great search. Never, to my knowledge, do animals other than ourselves suffer this unpredictable and unreasonable malady.

I have prescriptions for peace in the night too—a nonnarcotic, gentle way to slumber. Sleeplessness is not, apparently, a physical thing. Somewhere along the route through the day, nerves and tensions gather their forces and whirl the mind about in a frenzy. It's pointless to say, "Stop thinking—don't take your cares to bed with you." No one does it on purpose. The only way to divert the mind from its whirlwind course is to take it from its frenzied path and put it on something gentle and rhythmic and slightly wise. Ordinary prose reading won't do. You'll either pick a book so dull it diverts your thinking back to its original path, or you'll pick something so interesting, you'll be stimulated into further wakefulness. The subtle rhythms and wisdoms of poetry are what the boggled mind requires. Take Walt Whitman's "The Last Invocation" for a short prescription toward sleep.

At the last, tenderly,
From the walls of the powerful fortress'd house,
From the clasp of the knitted locks, from the keep of the well-
closed doors,
Let me be wafted.
Let me glide noiselessly forth;
With the key of softness unlock the locks—with a whisper,
Set ope the doors O soul.
Tenderly—be not impatient,
(Strong is your hold O mortal flesh,
Strong is your hold O love.)

Rhythm is important. Sleep comes to the music of words rising and falling in a softly persuasive arrangement. Something like a chant is good. Here's a simple prescription from Emily Dickinson that is short enough to be memorized and repeated over and over in the dark of the night. Read it and absorb the gentleness, and then take on the poet's sunny mind.

Besides the autumn poets sing
A few prosaic days
A little this side of the snow
And that side of the haze.

A few incisive mornings,
A few ascetic eyes,
Gone Mr. Bryant's goldenrod,
And Mr. Thomson's sheaves.

Still is the bustle in the brook,
Sealed are the spicy valves;
Mesmeric fingers softly touch
The eyes of many elves.

Perhaps a squirrel may remain,
My sentiments to share.
Grant me, O Lord, a sunny mind,
Thy windy will to bear!

With Dickinson, combine John Keats' "Sonnet to Sleep."

O soft embalmer of the still midnight!
Shutting, with careful fingers and benign,
Our gloom-pleased eyes, embowered from the light,
Enshaded in forgetfulness divine;
O soothest Sleep! if so it please thee, close,
In midst of this thine hymn, my willing eyes,
Or wait the amen, ere thy poppy throws
Around my bed its lulling charities;
Then save me, or the passed day will shine
Upon my pillow, breeding many woes;
Save me from curious conscience, that still lords
Its strength, for darkness burrowing like a mole;
Turn the key deftly in the oiled wards,
And seal the hushed casket of my soul.

Some sleep specialists have recommended calling serene scenes from remembered moments with nature to the mind's eye. A brook running through a field or forest, a sunset at sea, or maybe dappled things. Try Gerard Manley Hopkins' "Pied Beauty" on a sleepless night.

Glory be to God for Dappled things—
For skies of couple-color as brindled cow;
For rose-moles all in stipple upon trout that swim;
Fresh-firecoal chestnut-falls; finches' wings;
Landscape plotted and pieced—fold, fallow, and plough;
And all trades, their gear and tackle and trim.
All things, counter, original, spare, strange;
Whatever is fickle, freckled (who knows how?)
With swift, slow; sweet, sour; adazzle, dim;
He fathers-forth whose beauty is past change:
Praise him.

Meaning doesn't matter all the time, although sometimes it helps. If there is alliteration, soft sounds, images that relax thought, rhythm, it's all you need. The mind wants relief from confusion, anxiety, and tension. It's night and the mind doesn't want to think too deeply. Just enjoy the sound and the feel of the words and the simple thoughts the words evoke. It will work. If the thought in a poem is a sleep-connected thought, so much the better: then you have everything in one prescription. Read Robert Bridges' "Nightingales" at least twice and preferably repeat the dosage several times. Familiarity improves any poem.

Beautiful must be the mountains whence ye came,
And bright in the fruitful valleys the streams wherefrom
Ye learn your song:
Where are those starry woods? O might I wander there,
Among the flowers, which in that heavenly air
Bloom the year long!

Nay, barren are those mountains and spent the streams:
Our song is the voice of desire, that haunts our dreams,
A throe of the heart,
Whose pining visions dim, forbidden hopes profound,
No dying cadence nor long sigh can sound,
For all our art.

Alone, aloud in the raptured ear of men
We pour our dark nocturnal secret; and then,
As night is withdrawn
From these sweet-springing meads and bursting boughs of May,
Dream, while the innumerable choir of day
Welcome the dawn.

For those nights when sleep won't come no matter how you woo it, there's but one solution. Pretend to yourself that you'd rather be awake. By looking the other way, so to speak, you can sometimes trip sleep up and catch it, while you're about something different. I wrote a piece of light verse myself about this law of counter-reactives.

At night I spurn the coffee cup
And will not drink the brew,

Believing it will keep me up
Awake the whole night through.
But should I waken when the dawn
Has just begun to creep,
I drink a cup or two and yawn
And drift right back to sleep.

So, if it's really not working and the prescriptions thus far have failed, forget it—get up, make a pot of tea and take "Reveille" by A. E. Housman twice.

Wake: the silver dusk returning
Up the beach of darkness brims,
And the ship of sunrise burning
Strands upon the eastern rims.

Wake: the vaulted shadow shatters
Trampled to the floor it spanned,
And the tent of night in tatters
Straws the sky-pavilioned land.

Up, lad, up, 'tis late for lying:
Hear the drums of morning play;
Hark, the empty highways crying
"Who'll beyond the hills away?"

Towns and countries woo together,
Forelands beacon, belfries call;
Never lad that trod on leather
Lived to feast his heart with all.

Up, lad; thews that lie and cumber
Sunlit pallets never thrive;
Morns abed and daylight slumber
Were not meant for man alive.

Clay lies still, but blood's a rover;
Breath's a ware that will not keep.
Up, lad: when the journey's over
There'll be time enough to sleep.

And to really trip up sleep in this left-handed manner, take one more cup of tea with plenty of milk and add "Verses Written During a Sleepless Night" by Alexander Pushkin (translated by Babette Deutsch).

> Sleep evades me, there's no light:
> Darkness wraps the earth with slumber,
> Only weary tickings number
> The slow hours of the night.
> Parca, chattering woman-fashion,
> Night, that offers no compassion,
> Life that stirs like rustling mice—
> Why engage me in your Vice?
> Why the whispering insistence—
> Are you but the pale persistence
> Of a day departed twice?
> What black failures do you reckon?
> Do you prophesy or beckon?
> I would know whence you are sprung,
> I would study your dark tongue.

Finish the tea now and try writing some sleepless-night verse yourself. Then back to bed and the following prescriptions.

Aside from reflections on nature to court sleep, there are reflections on happy times, if they were times that weren't too wildly happy. Remembering a good time spent with someone compatible and feeling the pleasure again helps. Or, better still, reflect with the poet on a remembered moment of peace and fun. Then you have the rhythm, the luxury of well-chosen words combined with the event. There's Edna St. Vincent Millay's "Recuerdo" for this.

> We were very tired, we were very merry—
> We had gone back and forth all night on the ferry;
> It was bare and bright, and smelled like a stable—
> But we looked into a fire, we leaned across a table,
> We lay on a hill-top underneath the moon;
> And the whistles kept blowing, and the dawn came soon.
>
> We were very tired, we were very merry—
> We had gone back and forth all night on the ferry;
> And you ate an apple, and I ate a pear,
> From a dozen of each we had bought somewhere;

And the sky went wan, and the wind came cold,
And the sun rose dripping, a bucketful of gold.

We were very tired, we were very merry—
We had gone back and forth all night on the ferry.
We hailed, "Good-morrow, Mother!" to a shawl-covered head,
And bought a morning paper, which neither of us read;
And she wept, "God bless you!" for the apples and pears,
And we gave her all our money but our subway fares.

The darkest night will end. While it's upon you, forget the fury of thoughts that try to keep you awake and concentrate on the blackness of night. Then, turn on a dim light and take this prescription for sleep: "Credo" by Edwin Arlington Robinson.

I cannot find my way: there is no star
In all the shrouded heavens anywhere;
And there is not a whisper in the air
Of any living voice but one so far
That I can hear it only as a bar
Of lost, imperial music, played when fair
And angel fingers wove, and unaware,
Dead leaves to garlands where no roses are.
No, there is not a glimmer, nor a call,
For one that welcomes, welcomes when he fears,
The black and awful chaos of the night;
But through it all—above, beyond it all—
I know the far-sent message of the years,
I feel the coming glory of the light.

With "Credo" take "The West Wind" by John Masefield at least twice.

It's a warm wind, the west wind, full of birds' cries;
I never hear the west wind but tears are in my eyes.
For it comes from the west lands, the old brown hills,
And April's in the west wind, and daffodils.

It's a fine land, the west land, for hearts as tired as mine,
Apple orchards blossom there, and the air's like wine.

There is cool green grass there, where men may lie at rest,
And the thrushes are in song there, fluting from the nest.

"Will ye not come home, brother? ye have been long away,
It's April, and blossom time, and white is the may:
And bright is the sun, brother, and warm is the rain—
Will ye not come home, brother, home to us again?

The young corn is green, brother, where the rabbits run,
It's blue sky, and white clouds, and warm rain and sun.
It's song to a man's soul, brother, fire to a man's brain,
To hear the wild bees and see the merry spring again.

Larks are singing in the west, brother, above the green wheat
So will ye not come home, brother, and rest your tired feet?
I've a balm for bruised hearts, brother, sleep for aching eyes,"
Says the warm wind, the west wind, full of birds' cries.

It's the white road westwards is the road I must tread
To the green grass, the cool grass, and rest for heart and head,
To the violets and the warm hearts and the thrushes' song,
In the fine land, the west land, the land where I belong.

"Silver" by Walter de la Mare has sleep-producing sounds. It's short and rhythmic and can be memorized for repeating over and over during the night.

> Slowly, silently, now the moon
> Walks the night in her silver shoon;
> This way, and that, she peers, and sees
> Silver fruit upon silver trees;
> One by one the casements catch
> Her beams beneath the silvery thatch;
> Crouched in his kennel like a log,
> With paws of silver sleeps the dog;
> From their shadowy cote the white breasts peep
> Of doves in a silver-feathered sleep;
> A harvest mouse goes scampering by,
> With silver claws, and silver eye,
> And moveless fish in the water gleam,
> By silver reeds in a silver stream.

Poetry for Peace of Mind

The following poems are prescriptions that can be taken repeatedly. Like most sleeping potions, they should be taken one-half hour before bedtime. Make yourself comfortable and then let the sound of the words and rhythms sink gently into your consciousness. "To the Lady-bird" is an old English song.

Lady-bird! Lady-bird! Fly away home;
The field-mouse has gone to her nest,
The daisies have shut up their sweet sleepy eyes,
And the bees and the birds are at rest.

Lady-bird! Lady-bird! Fly away home;
The glow-worm is lighting her lamp,
The dew's falling fast, and your fine speckled wings
Will be wet with the close-clinging damp.

Lady-bird! Lady-bird! Fly away home;
The fairy-bells tinkle afar;
Make haste, or they'll catch you, and harness you fast
With a cobweb, to Oberon's car.

"Sea Fever" by John Masefield is rhythmic and restful.

I must go down to the seas again, to the lonely sea and the sky,
And all I ask is a tall ship and a star to steer her by,
And the wheel's kick and the wind's song and the white sail's
         shaking,
And a grey mist on the sea's face and a grey dawn breaking.

I must go down to the seas again, for the call of the running tide
Is a wild call and a clear call that may not be denied;
And all I ask is a windy day with the white clouds flying,
And the flung spray and the blown spume, and the sea-gulls
         crying.

I must go down to the seas again, to the vagrant gypsy life,
To the gull's way and the whale's way where the wind's like a
         whetted knife;
And all I ask is a merry yarn from a laughing fellow-rover,
And quiet sleep and a sweet dream when the long trick's over.

Now, for a sleepy softness, take "Velvet Shoes" by Elinor Wylie.

Let us walk in the white snow
In a soundless space;
With footsteps quiet and slow,
At a tranquil pace,
Under veils of white lace.

I shall go shod in silk,
And you in wool,
White as white cow's milk,
More beautiful
Than the breast of a gull.

We shall walk through the still town
In a windless peace;
We shall step upon the white down,
Upon silver fleece,
Upon softer than these.

We shall walk in velvet shoes:
Wherever we go
Silence will fall like dews
On white silence below.
We shall walk in the snow.

Add to it one capsule of "Wanderer's Night Song" by Johann Wolfgang von Goethe (translated by Henry Wadsworth Longfellow):

O'er all the hill tops
Is quiet now,
In all the tree tops
Hearest thou
Hardly a breath;
The birds are asleep in the trees;
Wait; soon like these
Thou too shall rest.

VII

To Break a Habit

I know of more than one person (including myself) who has used William Ernest Henley's "Invictus" as a tool to quit smoking. Every time I wanted a cigarette, some fifteen years ago, I repeated firmly to myself:

> It matters not how strait the gate,
> How charged with punishments the scroll,
> I am the master of my fate:
> I am the captain of my soul.

For the full poem, turn back to the Introduction.

A habit is a strange, possessive disease. Whatever it is, it wants to move in and rule the inner man. Smoking, drinking, and compulsive eating are the three major habit bogeymen, but there are, of course, a multitude of others from nail-biting to nagging. People who have bad habits like to fool themselves by thinking that, at any time, they can simply not do whatever it is they are doing. But anyone who has struggled with the suppression of a habit knows that giving it up has elements of genuine pain. The first five days of abstinence from smoking are a period filled with real withdrawal symptoms. Your head is light, your temper is hair-triggered and your normally intelligent mind is obsessed by the thought of a cigarette until there's no room for any other thought. Even later on, when there *are* periods when you've forgotten about smoking, the old yearning dragon can breathe its fire of longing all over you at an odd, unexpected moment. This is when Henley helps tremendously. I can't count the hundreds of times I put down the urge to smoke by saying firmly, "I *am* the master of my fate. I *am* the captain of my soul."

Breaking a habit takes real motivation. The first step is to make it absolutely clear to yourself that the death of this particular thing is of great importance to you. Spend a lot of time thinking about it before you really go at it. If it's smoking, for example, smoke furiously for a week. Examine your feelings when you smoke. Think how much better off you will be when you quit. Know that you *can* and *will* be able to do it. Prepare to find it painful and face down the fear of deprivation, knowing you can grind your way through five days. After five days are over, the longing will lessen and the feeling of accomplishment will be so great, everything else will become less and less disturbing. From the moment you have put out your last cigarette, start using the prescriptions that follow, regularly. At every urge to return to the habit, take several doses of "Invictus" or any of the poems selected here. Your mind will obey if your determination is strong. Breaking a habit is, after all, only a reversal of what it took to start the habit in the beginning. Habits are tenacious thoughts that time and repetition put securely into the mind. Undo them then, by reversing the process and putting into the mind (over and over again) new words that will replace them.

To help lessen the painful first moments involved in breaking a deeply imbedded habit, try this prescription by Emily Dickinson:

> After great pain a formal feeling comes—
> The nerves sit ceremonious like tombs;
> The stiff Heart questions—was it He that bore?
> And yesterday—or centuries before?
>
> The feet mechanical
> Go round a wooden way
> Of ground or air or Ought, regardless grown,
> A quartz contentment like a stone.

This is the hour of lead
Remembered if outlived,
As freezing persons recollect the snow—
First chill, then stupor, then the letting go.

Anyone who has freed himself from the clawing tentacles of a habit knows that "the feet mechanical go round" and that there is "a quartz contentment like a stone." But it *is* followed by the "chill, then stupor, then the *letting go*."

If you absorb yourself with the words of the following prescription at a moment of crisis in breaking a habit, you will begin to see the dark angel as the beleaguering demon that has tried to be your master. Use the first two lines of the last verse—as the last lines of "Invictus" are used. Memorize them and keep them on hand and they will work like a shield when the old longing tries to stab you. "The Dark Angel" is by Lionel Johnson.

Dark angel, with thine aching lust
To rid the world of penitence:
Malicious Angel, who still dost
My soul such subtile violence!

Because of thee, no thought, no thing
Abides for me undesecrate:
Dark Angel, ever on the wing,
Who never reachest me too late!

When music sounds, then changest thou
Its silvery to a sultry fire:
Nor will thine envious heart allow
Delight untortured by desire.

Through thee, the gracious Muses turn
To Furies, O mine Enemy!
And all the things of beauty burn
With flames of evil ecstasy.

Because of thee, the land of dreams
Becomes a gathering place of fears:
Until tormented slumber seems
One vehemence of useless tears.

When sunlight glows upon the flowers,
Or ripples down the dancing sea:
Thou, with thy troop of passionate powers,
Beleaguerest, bewilderest me.

Within the breath of autumn woods,
Within the winter silences:
Thy venomous spirit stirs and broods,
O master of impieties!

The ardour of red flame is thine,
And thine the steely soul of ice;
Thou poisonest the fair design
Of nature, with unfair device.

Apples of ashes, golden bright;
Waters of bitterness, how sweet!
O banquet of a foul delight,
Prepared by thee, dark Paraclete.

Thou art the whisper in the gloom,
The hinting tone, the haunting laugh:
Thou art the adorner of my tomb,
The minstrel of mine epitaph.

I fight thee, in the Holy Name!
Yet, what thou dost, is what God saith:
Tempter! should I escape thy flame,
Thou wilt have helped my soul from Death:

The second Death, that never dies,
That cannot die, when time is dead:
Live Death, wherein the lost soul cries,
Eternally uncomforted.

Dark Angel, with thine aching lust!
Of two defeats, of two despairs:
Less dread, a change to drifting dust,
Than thine eternity of cares.

Do what thou wilt, thou shalt not so,
Dark Angel, triumph over me:

> Lonely, unto the lone I go;
> Divine, to the Divinity.

Habits are insidious little demons that rise up and attack you at moments when you feel secure in believing you've licked them forever. If there's a prescription in this collection that works particularly well for you, copy it and carry it with you wherever you go. Then you won't be caught without help at a critical moment.

"The Village Atheist" by Edgar Lee Masters has a determination-building aspect about it.

> Ye young debaters over the doctrine
> Of the soul's immortality,
> I who lie here was the village atheist,
> Talkative, contentious, versed in the arguments
> Of the infidels.
> But through a long sickness
> Coughing myself to death
> I read the Upanishads and the poetry of Jesus.
> And they lighted a torch of hope and intuition
> And desire which the Shadow,
> Leading me swiftly through the caverns of darkness,
> Could not extinguish.
> Listen to me, ye who live in the senses
> And think through the senses only:
> Immortality is not a gift,
> Immortality is an achievement,
> And only those who strive mightily
> Shall possess it.

There is no achievement quite like the successful breaking of a habit. There are many clichés about the inability of a reformed smoker or drinker to keep quiet on the subject. People should be more compassionate and let him brag—it was a massive accomplishment! Possession of that feeling is the reward that keeps dangling before you as you fight your way toward freedom. It's the promise of a ball of gold that keeps the reforming soul on the track. Take Stephen Crane's "A Ball of Gold" every time you think you may be losing sight of your goal.

A man saw a ball of gold in the sky:
He climbed for it,
And eventually he achieved it—
It was clay.

Now this is the strange part:
When the man went to the earth
And looked again,
Lo, there was the ball of gold.
It was a ball of gold.
Ay, by the heavens, it was a ball of gold.

It helps to think of your habit as something repulsive. You thought your way into becoming its slave, so it's not strange to find you can think your way free. A prescription to help train your mind toward contempt of your habit is W. H. Davies' "The White Monster." Keep the thought of the habit in your mind as you read.

Last night I saw the monster near; the big
White monster that was like a lazy slug,
That hovered in the air, not far away,
As quiet as the black hawk seen by day.
I saw it turn its body round about,
And look my way; I saw its big fat snout
Turn straight towards my face, till I was one
In coldness with that statue made of stone,
The one-armed sailor seen upon my right—
With no more power than he to offer fight;
The great white monster slug that, even then,
Killed women, children and defenseless men.
But soon its venom was discharged, and it,
Knowing it had no more the power to spit
Death on the most defenseless English folk,
Let out a large, thick cloud of its own smoke;
And when the smoke had cleared away from there,
I saw no sign of my monster near;
And nothing but the stars to give alarm—
That never did the earth a moment's harm.
Oh, it was strange to see a thing like jelly,

An ugly boneless thing all black and belly,
Among the peaceful stars—that should have been
A mile deep in the sea, and never seen:
A big, fat, lazy slug that, even then,
Killed women, children and defenseless men.

In the same vein, Alexander Pope wrote of "Vice":

Vice is a monster of so frightful mien,
As to be hated, needs but to be seen;
Yet seen too oft, familiar with her face,
We first endure, then pity, then embrace.

Alcoholism has become one of the greatest social problems of our time. For many, the force of habit keeps them drinking against their better judgment. Society has made it not only acceptable, but almost necessary. Although alcoholism is a disease and one I wouldn't pretend could be cured with the simple potion of a poem, I have seen alcoholics in poetry therapy at Pilgrim State Hospital who are ready to admit that a poem gave them the strength to help solve their problem. A prescription for this, or for any habit, is Edwin Arlington Robinson's "Miniver Cheevy." It's an insight into a human condition in all of us some of the time and in some of us all of the time. Although it ends on a hopeless note, its very hopelessness is hopeful to one who recognizes the message it bears. No matter how bound by habit we may be, we don't have to let it defeat us, or let life defeat us as it defeated Miniver.

Miniver Cheevy, child of scorn,
Grew lean while he assailed the seasons;
He wept that he was ever born,
And he had reasons.

Miniver loved the days of old
When swords were bright and steeds were prancing;
The vision of a warrior bold
Would set him dancing.

Miniver sighed for what was not,
And dreamed, and rested from his labors;

He dreamed of Thebes and Camelot,
And Priam's neighbors.

Miniver mourned the ripe renown
That made so many a name so fragrant;
He mourned Romance, now on the town,
And Art, a vagrant.

Miniver loved the Medici,
Albeit he had never seen one;
He would have sinned incessantly
Could he have been one.

Miniver cursed the commonplace,
And eyed a khaki suit with loathing;
He missed the medieval grace
Of iron clothing.

Miniver scorned the gold he sought,
But sore annoyed was he without it;
Miniver thought, and thought, and thought,
And thought about it.

Miniver Cheevy, born too late,
Scratched his head and kept on thinking;
Miniver coughed and called it fate,
And kept on drinking.

Another prescription by the same poet also helped work some
bright miracles at Pilgrim State Hospital. On first reading it doesn't
seem to apply to habit breaking, but in "Reuben Bright" the alco-
holic patients in Sidney Farcas's group saw the tearing down of the
slaughter house as synonymous with tearing down their own hang-
ups. The phrase, "We'll have to tear down the slaughter house,"
became a stock one when they worked on their problems in group
therapy.

Because he was a butcher and thereby
Did earn an honest living (and did right)
I would not have you think that Reuben Bright
Was any more a brute than you or I;
For when they told him that his wife must die,

He stared at them and shook with grief and fright,
And cried like a great baby half that night,
And made the woman cry to see him cry.
And after she was dead, and he had paid
The singers and the sexton and the rest,
He packed a lot of things that she had made
Most mournfully away in an old chest
Of hers, and put some chopped-up cedar boughs
In with them, and tore down the slaughter house.

Mix Reuben with a capsule of "Do You Fear the Wind?" by Hamlin Garland.

> Do you fear the force of the wind,
> The slash of the rain?
> Go face them and fight them,
> Be savage again.
> Go hungry and cold like the wolf,
> Go wade like the crane:
> The palms of your hands will thicken,
> The skin of your cheek will tan,
> You'll grow ragged and weary and swarthy,
> But you'll walk like a man!

Add two short draughts of "The Oak" by Alfred, Lord Tennyson.

> Live thy Life,
> Young and old,
> Like yon oak,
> Bright in spring,
> Living gold;
>
> Summer-rich
> Then; and then
> Autumn-changed,
> Soberer-hued
> Gold again.
>
> All his leaves
> Fallen at length,

Look, he stands,
Trunk and bough,
Naked strength.

Everyone wants a panacea. Everyone wants liberty without strife. But when the enemy has been put down, the relief and sense of fulfillment is so great one wonders why the struggle itself wasn't an overwhelming joy. Arthur Hugh Clough's "Say Not the Struggle" is a helpful prescription for putting down the enemy of habit.

Say not the struggle nought availeth
The labor and the wounds are vain,
The enemy faints not, nor faileth,
And as things have been they remain.

If hopes were dupes, fears may be liars;
It may be, in yon smoke concealed,
Your comrades chase e'en now the fliers,
And, but for you, possess the field.

For while the tired waves, vainly breaking,
Seem here no painful inch to gain,
Far back, through creeks and inlets making,
Comes silent, flooding in, the main.

And not by eastern windows only,
When daylight comes, comes in the light,
In front, the sun climbs slow, how slowly,
But westward, look, the land is bright.

When you want to break a habit, you have to believe you *can* and *will* do it, and call on all your inner resources to join you on the battlefield.

The next prescription for habit breaking is from "Divine Comedy" by Henry Wadsworth Longfellow. Its message is one of faith and lack of shame in admitting a burden and reaching for help in laying it down.

Oft have I seen at some Cathedral door
A laborer, pausing in the dust and heat,

Lay down his burden, and with reverent feet
Enter, and cross himself, and on the floor
Kneel to repeat his paternoster o'er;
Far off the noises of the world retreat;
The loud vociferations of the street
Become an undistinguishable roar.
So, as I enter here from day to day,
And leave my burden at this minster gate,
Kneeling in prayer, and not ashamed to pray,
The tumult of the time disconsolate
To inarticulate murmurs dies away,
While the eternal ages watch and wait.

Poetry is tremendously personal. Whatever the poet may have wanted us to believe, we often read our own interpretations into his thinking. One of the great powers of the poem is its ability to fit the need of the reader at a given moment. If there is one prescription, among these last selections, that fits you best or helps strengthen your willpower, make it your own. Learn it. Lean on it. Poetry will never hurt you. Habits are like the little brown autumn burrs that lie by the roadside and catch your clothing as you pass. They are quick to take hold, and the devil himself to ungrip; but determination, persistence, and the reward of achievement hanging within your reach will tear them down.

When doubtful of your ability to kick a bad habit, take a dose of "It Couldn't Be Done" by Edgar A. Guest.

Somebody said that it couldn't be done,
    But he with a chuckle replied
That "maybe it couldn't," but he would be one
    Who wouldn't say so till he'd tried.
So he buckled right in with the trace of a grin
    On his face. If he worried he hid it.
He started to sing as he tackled the thing
    That couldn't be done, and he did it.

Somebody scoffed: "Oh, you'll never do that;
    At least no one has done it";
But he took off his coat and he took off his hat,

And the first thing we knew he'd begun it.
With a lift of his chin and a bit of a grin,
　　Without any doubting or quiddit,
He started to sing as he tackled the thing
　　That couldn't be done, and he did it.

There are thousands to tell you it cannot be done,
　　There are thousands to prophesy failure;
There are thousands to point out to you, one by one,
　　The dangers that wait to assail you.
But just buckle in with a bit of a grin,
　　Just take off your coat and go to it;
Just start to sing as you tackle the thing
　　That "cannot be done," and you'll do it.

To help strengthen your resolve when discouragement plagues you and you're ready to throw in the towel, add a measure of "The Quitter," by an unknown poet.

It ain't the failures he may meet
　　That keeps a man from winnin'
It's the discouragement complete
　　That blocks a new beginnin';
You want to quit your habits bad,
　　And, when the shadows flittin'
Make life seem worthless an' sad,
　　You want to quit your quittin'!

You want to quit a-layin' down
　　An' sayin' hope is over,
Because the fields are bare an' brown
　　Where once we lived in clover.
When jolted from the water cart
　　It's painful to be hittin'
The earth; but make another start.
　　Cheer up, an' quit your quittin'!

Although the game seems rather stiff,
　　Don't be a doleful doubter;
There's always one more innin' if

You're not a down-and-outer.
But fortune's pretty sure to flee
From folks content with sittin'
Around an' sayin' life's N.G.
You've got to quit your quittin'!

Finally, take liberal doses of "Will" by Ella Wheeler Wilcox.

There is no chance, no destiny, no fate,
Can circumvent or hinder or control
The firm resolve of a determined soul.
Gifts count for nothing; will alone is great;
All things give way before it, soon or late.
What obstacle can stay the mighty force
Of the sea-seeking river in its course,
Or cause the ascending orb of day to wait?

Each wellborn soul must win what it deserves.
Let the fool prate of luck. The fortunate
Is he whose earnest purpose never swerves,
Whose slightest action or inaction serves
The one great aim. Why, even Death stands still,
And waits an hour sometimes for such a will.

VIII
Failure

I might have done well to title this chapter "Success," for of all human experiences it is perhaps the hardest to take. The world is full of people who avoid success assiduously, even though possessed of talents and abilities that would move them to high places—if they pursued them. One woman I know spent thirty years writing, but never made any attempt to sell her output. Finally, she was challenged by a person who saw through her disguise. "Why," she asked, "aren't you sending your work to publishers?"

The writer, who thought she understood some of the workings of her inner self, said, "I guess that I'm afraid that I'll have to prove myself. I'm afraid that if I offer it for publication, I'll fail."

"Turn the coin over," her friend said, "and look at the other side. Couldn't you also be afraid that you'll succeed? Don't forget, the groove you've been in all these years has been a comfortable one. At least, it's familiar and one you can deal with. If you step out of your own image, you'll have new challenges to meet. Think about it," she added, "and see if there isn't some truth there."

The writer thought about it very intently and recognized its sense. She began to send her work out for publication. She is now a very successful full-time free-lance writer.

Everybody fails some of the time. Even the first hitter, up at bat, strikes out now and then. To succeed some of the time is about all anyone can ask. The rest of the time we need support in not letting our failures get us too far down. One of the many reasons failure occurs is because we aim too high. It's pointless to place demands on yourself that you can't really meet. I know a man who has spent a lifetime hating himself for not being able to become the saintly person his mother was. Deeply religious, she apparently had no vices, and never complained; she met life with serene fortitude and never knuckled under. Her standards were too high—her son could never reach her plateau. Needing her approval, he was frustrated throughout life by a continuous sense of failure.

Another woman friend had a mother who held a Ph.D. Once again, the standard—this time intellectual rather than moral—was too high. She finally quit high school after five years with four F's and one C. She too, spent a lifetime with the frustration of continual failure. However, it was an image she was used to seeing. Whether she liked it or not, she was familiar and comfortable in the groove and she made no real effort to change her condition.

Many of us try to quit smoking and fail, aim for a promotion and miss it, take a test and flunk it, or bake a cake and burn it. Failures, somewhere along the way, seem to be required; perhaps only to give more flavor to success when it does arrive. You can't discuss failure without bringing in its opposite, success.

The woman writer mentioned in the beginning of this chapter had serious bouts with the success syndrome before she conditioned herself to accept the fact that she was doing well professionally. Her first sales filled her at once with elation and joy, and terrible attacks of anxiety later. It always happened. She persevered, however, and finally succeeded in putting down the waves of panic that each success brought. Success meant changing her self-image and the panic was caused by the unfamiliar territory she found herself afoot in.

The same thing happened to a person who had been told as a child that she was tone-deaf. In school, instead of helping her to learn her music, the teachers and students begged her not to sing because she was throwing off others in the chorus. Years later, a voice teacher proved to her that tonal qualities *can* be learned. He undertook teaching her to get on pitch. She was suddenly confronted with the success of hitting notes precisely and correctly. For days before each lesson she became unnerved, filled with strange anxieties, until she realized she was doing successfully something

Poetry for Peace of Mind

that she had been told repeatedly she couldn't do. She'd had the nerve to set foot on forbidden ground!

The poem prescriptions collected here will exorcise the ghosts of both failure and success. They will get you past points of failure and ease you toward your next success. If you've really flubbed things, there's nothing much you can do but accept the fact and renew your faith in yourself and your ability to make the grade on the next hill. The first prescription is from "Ode" by Arthur William Edgar O'Shaughnessy. "The world," the poet said, "was created out of the dreams and efforts of all the ages, despite the ups and downs of the struggle to conquer and create."

> We are the music-makers,
> And we are the dreamers of dreams,
> Wandering by lone sea-breakers,
> And sitting by desolate streams;
> World-losers and world-forsakers,
> On whom the pale moon gleams:
> Yet we are the movers and shakers
> Of the world forever, it seems.
>
> With wonderful deathless ditties
> We build up the world's great cities,
> And out of a fabulous story
> We fashion an empire's glory:
> One man with a dream, at pleasure,
> Shall go forth and conquer a crown;
> And three with a new song's measure
> Can trample an empire down.
>
> We, in the ages lying
> In the buried past of the earth,
> Built Nineveh with our sighing,
> And Babel itself with our mirth;
> And o'erthrew them with prophesying
> To the old of the new world's worth;
> For each age is a dream that is dying,
> Or one that is coming to birth.

There is comfort in knowing that even the greatest leaders and artists of the past have failed and continued to fail throughout their lives. All the glorious achievements of men have crept painfully into their existence as a result of failures. Edison had to make a great many mistakes before it was possible for him to do one thing correctly. No really wonderful result ever burst full-bloom from a first attempt. It takes drive and determination to succeed, and it also takes joy in the doing. The next prescription is a poem by Robert Bridges entitled "To L.B.C.L.M."

> I love all beauteous things,
> I seek and adore them;
> God hath no better praise,
> And man in his hasty days
> Is honoured for them.
>
> I too will something make
> And joy in the making;
> Altho' to-morrow it seem
> Like the empty words of a dream
> Remembered on waking.

Because it's a small capsule, take it twice, and add at least one dose of "The Long Hill" by Sara Teasdale.

> I must have passed the crest a while ago
> And now I am going down—
> Strange to have crossed the crest and not to know,
> But the brambles were always catching the hem of my gown.
>
> All the morning I thought how proud I should be
> To stand there straight as a queen,
> Wrapped in the wind and the sun, and the world under me—
> But the air was dull, there was little I could have seen.
>
> It was nearly level along the beaten track
> And the brambles caught in my gown—
> But it's no use now to think of turning back,
> The rest of the way will be only going down.

Because of the personal quality of poetry, picking it out for others is difficult. We read into poems what we want to be there. The poet talks in images and metaphors and makes comparisons. But in a good poem, the light of a general idea comes through. Now, try Herman Melville's "Art."

> In placid hours well pleased we dream
> Of many a brave embodied scheme.
> But form to lend, pulsed life create,
> What unlike things must meet and mate;
> A flame to melt—a wind to freeze;
> Sad patience—joyous energies;
> Humility—yet pride and scorn;
> Instinct and study; love and hate;
> Audacity—reverence. These must mate
> And fuse with Jacob's mystic heart,
> To wrestle with the angel—Art.

Another poet who wrestled with the angel art was Dylan Thomas. In his poem "In My Craft or Sullen Art" he tells why he must pursue his muse and whip failure—simply because he must.

> In my craft or sullen art
> Exercised in the still night
> When only the moon rages
> And the lovers lie abed
> With all their griefs in their arms,
> I labor by singing light
> Not for ambition or bread
> Or the strut and trade of charms
> On the ivory stages
> But for the common wages
> Of their most secret heart.
>
> Not for the proud man apart
> From the raging moon I write
> On these spindrift pages
> Nor for the towering dead
> With their nightingales and psalms

But for the lovers, their arms
Round the griefs of the ages,
Who pay no praise or wages
Nor heed my craft or art.

Norman Rockwell once told me of how he painted—how he worked over and over a drawing and, when it was finally done, packed it up for the publisher and prayed. "Do you mean that you still worry about your work being accepted?" I asked, aghast. It was his turn to be amazed. Even after years of tremendous success, bearing a name that one would think could not be said in the same breath with failure, he still sweated out the acceptance of his work. All creative people are familiar with the waves of despair that sweep in during the birthing of a new idea.

Not all failure, however, is related to work or art. Sometimes we fail in friendship or love. At these times, we have to recall how fleeting everything is and how good the good can be, in spite of its passing. This prescription will help you; it's by Wilfrid Scawen Blunt, "To One Who Would Make a Confession."

Oh! leave the past to bury its own dead.
The past is naught to us, the present all.
What need of last year's leaves to strew Love's bed?
What need of ghosts to grace a festival?
I would not, if I could, those days recall,
Those days not ours. For us the feast is spread,
The lamps are lit, and music plays withal.
Then let us love and leave the rest unsaid.
This island is our home. Around it roar
Great gulfs and oceans, channels, straits, and seas.
What matter in what wreck we reached the shore,
So we both reached it? We can mock at these.
Oh! leave the Past, if Past indeed there be.
I would not know it. I would know but thee.

A charming, tongue-in-cheek prescription for success comes next from Sir W. S. Gilbert. It's "Sir Joseph's Song," from *H.M.S. Pinafore*, and it's always a good one to take in the teeth of failure.

When I was a lad I served a term
As office boy to an attorney's firm.
I cleaned the windows and I swept the floor,
And I polished up the handle of the big front door.
I polished up that handle so carefullee
That now I am the Ruler of the Queen's Navee!

As office boy I made such a mark
That they gave me the post of a junior clerk.
I served the writs with a smile so bland,
And I copied all the letters in a big round hand—
I copied all the letters in a hand so free,
That now I am the Ruler of the Queen's Navee!

In serving writs I made such a name
That an articled clerk I soon became;
I wore clean collars and a brand new suit
For the pass examination at the Institute,
And that pass examination did so well for me,
That now I am the ruler of the Queen's Navee!

Of legal knowledge I acquired such a grip
That they took me into the partnership,
And that junior partnership, I ween,
Was the only ship I ever had seen.
But that kind of ship so suited me,
That now I am the Ruler of the Queen's Navee!

I grew so rich that I was sent
By a pocket borough into Parliament.
I always voted at my party's call,
And never thought of thinking for myself at all.
I thought so little they rewarded me
By making me the Ruler of the Queen's Navee!

Now landsmen all, whoever you may be
If you want to rise to the top of the tree,
If your soul isn't fettered to an office stool,
Be careful to be guided by this golden rule—
Stick close to your desks and never go to sea,
And you all may be rulers of the Queen's Navee!

Failure

Emily Dickinson never knew success while she lived. However, if the immortality she pursued and longed for has come to her after all, she now knows the fullest measure of success. She managed neatly to duck the agonies of failure throughout her life by simply not allowing its entrance. Perhaps sometimes she wished that others could hear her singing, but never once did she make any attempt to have her poems published. Either failure or success so paralyzed her that she hid from the world in total seclusion and wrote out her more than a thousand poems in a cloak of invisibility.

So often, when a man has failed, he has but to look about him a little more closely. He will find more successes than he thought he had, in areas he had forgotten. Success, so called, doesn't always bring undiluted happiness. Most often, whatever it is we call happiness comes, as "Peanuts" points out, in small things like a warm puppy. Henry Howard, Earl of Surrey, wrote in the sixteenth century of "The Means to Attain Happy Life."

> Martial, the things that do attain
> The happy life be these, I find:
> The riches left, not got with pain;
> The fruitful ground, the quiet mind;
>
> The equal friend; no grudge, no strife;
> No charge of rule, nor governance;
> Without disease, the healthful life;
> The household of continuance;
>
> The mean diet, no delicate fare;
> True wisdom joined with simpleness;
> The night discharged of all care,
> Where wine the wit may not oppress:
>
> The faithful wife, without debate;
> Such sleeps as may beguile the night;
> Contented with thine own estate,
> Ne wish for death, ne fear his might.

To re-establish a comfortable sense of values and to take away the pressure, the frustration, and the pain of failure, try this prescription, "The Return" by Edna St. Vincent Millay.

Earth does not understand her child,
Who from the loud gregarious town
Returns, depleted and defiled,
To the still woods, to fling him down.

Earth cannot count the sons she bore:
The wounded lynx, the wounded man
Come trailing blood unto her door;
She shelters both as best she can.

But she is early up and out,
To trim the year or strip its bones;
She has no time to stand about
Talking of him in undertones

Who has no aim but to forget,
Be left in peace, by lying thus
For days, for years, for centuries yet,
Unshaven and anonymous;

Who, marked for failure, dulled by grief,
Has traded in his wife and friend
For this warm ledge, this alder leaf;
Comfort that does not comprehend.

Next, take a dose of the philosophy of Ogden Nash in "Kindly Unhitch That Star, Buddy."

I hardly suppose I know anybody who wouldn't rather be a success than a failure.
Just as I suppose every piece of crabgrass in the garden would rather be an azalea,
And in celestial circles all the run-of-the-mill angels would rather be archangels or at least cherubim and seraphim.
And in the legal world all the little process-servers hope to grow up into great big baliffim and sheriffim.
Indeed, everybody wants to be a wow,
But not everybody knows exactly how.
Some people think they will eventually wear diamonds instead of rhinestones
Only by everlastingly keeping their noses to their ghrinestones.

Failure

And other people think they will be able to put in more time at
        Palm Beach and the Ritz
By not paying too much attention to attendance at the office, but
        rather in being brilliant by starts and fits.
Some people after a full day's work sit up all night getting a
        college education by correspondence,
While others seem to think they'll get just as far by devoting
        their evenings to the study of the difference in
        temperament between brunettance and blondance.
Some stake theirs all on luck,
And others put their faith in their ability to pass the buck.
In short, the world is filled with people trying to achieve success,
And half of them think they'll get it by saying No, and half of
        them by saying Yes,
And if all the ones who say No said Yes, and vice versa, such is
        the fate of humanity that ninety-nine per cent of them
        still wouldn't be any better off than they were before.
Which perhaps is just as well because if everybody was a success,
        nobody could be contemptuous of anybody else and
        everybody would start in all over again trying to be a
        bigger success than everybody else so they would
        have somebody to be contemptuous of and so on
        forevermore,
Because when people start hitching their wagons to a star,
That's the way they are.

And the last prescription that places values where they belong,
on things that last, "A Thing of Beauty" by John Keats.

    A thing of beauty is a joy forever:
    Its loveliness increases; it will never
    Pass into nothingness; but still will keep
    A bower quiet for us, and a sleep
    Full of sweet dreams, and health, and quiet breathing.
    Therefore, on every morrow, are we wreathing
    A flowery band to bind us to the earth,
    Spite of despondence, of the inhuman dearth
    Of noble natures, of the gloomy days,
    Of all the unhealthy and o'er-darkened ways

Made for our searching: yes, in spite of all,
Some shape of beauty moves away the pall
From our dark spirits. Such the sun, the moon,
Trees old and young, sprouting a shady boon
For simple sheep; and such are daffodils
With the green world they live in; and clear rills
That for themselves a cooling covert make
'Gainst the hot season; the mid-forest brake,
Rich with a sprinkling of fair musk-rose blooms:
And such too is the grandeur of the dooms
We have imagined for the mighty dead;
All lovely tales that we have heard or read:
And endless fountain of immortal drink,
Pouring unto us from the heaven's brink.
Nor do we merely feel these essences
For one short hour; no, even as the trees
That whisper round a temple become soon
Dear as the temple's self, so does the moon,
The passion poesy, glories infinite,
Haunt us till they become a cheering light
Unto our souls, and bound to us so fast,
That, whether there be shine, or gloom o'ercast,
They alway must be with us, or we die.

IX

To Sustain Joy

Not all prescriptions are preventative or curative. Some serve to sustain a mood. Most of these poem prescriptions are double-edged, because human emotions are double-edged. You can't have failure without success; you can't have fear without tension; depression gets all mixed up with dependency and guilt or fatigue. And you can't have any negative emotion without its opposite—joy. Or contentment—which is a quiet joy. People are made up of varying moods and feelings, and most of us are constantly in search of joy in any of its degrees. Once we have it, we don't want to let it go.

One of the shortest routes to a swift sense of joy is in humor. For a brief moment, everything falls in place. Many times the opposite of joy is man-made and constructed from the lack of humorous thinking. Our humorists and comedians are great therapists. Whatever weight one is carrying (whether for a real or imagined cause), a funny bit of business or an amusing story will snap us out of it, if only for a moment. Light verse does a remarkable job. Most light-verse makers work on the multi-subjects of the human condition. If viewed objectively, people can be very funny, and situations that are quite painful at the time of their happening are often hilarious when viewed in retrospect.

One of the great poetic wits of this century was Dorothy Parker. Unfortunately, her output wasn't large, but each poem was a brilliant gem. You won't be able to suppress a surge of joy when you recognize yourself in her "Portrait of the Artist." This is all of us at one time or another.

Oh, lead me to a quiet cell
Where never footfall rankles,
And bar the windows passing well,
And gyve my wrists and ankles.

Oh, wrap my eyes with linen fair,
With hempen cord go bind me,
And of your mercy, leave me there,
Nor tell them where to find me.

Oh, lock the portals as you go,
And see its bolts be double . . .
Come back in half an hour or so,
And I will be in trouble.

Another great female contributor to joy is Phyllis McGinley. She, too, takes the human situation, lightens it, stirs in wit and rhyme and rhythm, and dishes out all the ingredients that sustain joy. You see yourself in her verse, and, magically, it lightens your load. Anything you can laugh at loses its power to hurt. Take "The Female of the Species Is Hardier Than the Male" to keep a happy sense of elation up where it belongs.

Oliver Ames is a stalwart man,
Whose strength is a gushing fountain.
With a nonchalant smile he swims his mile
Or conquers the savage mountain.
Girded for sport, he holds the fort
When the rivals are round him dropping,
But clear the deck
For a Total Wreck
Whenever I take him shopping.

Oliver is winded, Oliver's awry.
He clutches at the counters and he plucks at his tie.
On his overheated face
There's a weary sort of frown,
And he's looking for a place
Where he can just sit down.
And he mops at his brow

And he tugs at his cuff,
And vows a mighty vow
That he's had about enough.

Now a sturdy oak is Oliver Ames,
While I'm the ivy, twining.
I make no claims for my skill at games
And I exercise best, reclining.
But when I'm out on a shopping bout
Where the glittering price tags leer up,
Stouter and bolder,
It's always my shoulder
That bolsters my frazzled dear up.

Saturday is young yet; I'm going like a breeze.
But Oliver is glassy-eyed and sagging at the knees.
We've only looked at draperies,
We've only stormed the lifts
For silverware and naperies
And half a dozen gifts;
We've only searched the basements
For underwear and rugs
And curtains for our casements,
And copper water jugs.

And still the time is ample
For doing this and that.
I want to match a sample,
I want to buy a hat.
I want to see the furniture that decks the Model House.
But Oliver is muttering the mutters of a spouse,
And his temper goes a soaring
While his metatarsals sink
And he totters homeward roaring
For a pillow and a drink.

Oh, Delilah might have saved herself that legendary cropping
If she'd only taken Samson on a Saturday of Shopping.

As a small afterthought, you might add one of my verses, called
"Blind Spot."

Riddles of government he solves,
And instinctively he knows
How martial strategy applies
And how to prune a rose.

His intellect is quick and keen
In judging current stocks,
But he simply cannot figure out
In which drawer I store his socks.

Marriage is an open meadow with acres and acres of opportunity for poems of wit and joy. All the little difficulties in a good marriage are universal and laughable if handled properly, and serve to bind the couple more closely. This applies to the courting couple, too, or any man-woman relationship. Here's a prescription from Dorothy Parker again: "One Perfect Rose."

A single flow'r he sent me, since we met.
All tenderly his messenger he chose;
Deep-hearted, pure, with scented dew still wet—
One perfect rose.

I knew the language of the floweret;
"My fragile leaves" it said, "his heart enclose."
Love long has taken for his amulet
One perfect rose.

Why is it no one ever sent me yet
One perfect limousine, do you suppose?
Ah no, it's always just my luck to get
One perfect rose.

With that, take a quick dose of another of Dorothy Parker's poems, "Experience."

Some men break your heart in two,
Some men fawn and flatter
Some men never look at you;
And that cleans up the matter.

Everyone who has a child knows about the millions of frustrations mixed with the joys of parenthood. One of today's great versifying joy-makers is Richard Armour. Try keeping the joy level up during moments of parental crisis with "On His Marks."

Junior's just a little tot,
But handy with a pen.
He writes on walls, as soon as not,
In living room and den.

Junior's very small, but still,
With crayon and with paint,
He daubs the wall with right good will,
Although we say he mayn't.

Junior scrawls, despite his age,
With pencilings unstinted.
He can deface the title page
Of any book that's printed.

Junior's destined to embark
On some career quite steady.
I'm certain he will make his mark;
In fact, he has already.

A poem of mine that can be added to this is called "Physical Fitness."

That sturdy little son of mine
Is muscular and fit—
Twenty push-ups he can do
And not make much of it.

But bending down just once a day
Is too much of a chore
If it's involved with picking up
His clothing off the floor.

Another one of mine is a prescription for joy-bolstering later in life.

Retribution often is
In itself a goal.
At other times it merely helps
To soothe a mother's soul.

I'd like to tell my daughter,
But propriety forbids,
What good it does me just to hear
Her holler at *her* kids!

There are also more serious aspects to joy. Sometimes joy almost seems to attack—as anxiety and boredom do. There are wild moments of joy available in the perfect June day, the blazing sunset over a mountain ridge or an open bay. Autumn has days that bring unmeasurable joy. Even a great snowstorm can fill you with joy and the sense of completeness in nature. Emily Dickinson knew all about these moments:

I taste a liquor never brewed,
From tankards scooped in pearl;
Not all the vats upon the Rhine
Yield such an alcohol!

Inebriate of air am I,
And debauchee of dew,
Reeling, through endless summer days,
From inns of molten blue.

When landlords turn, the drunken bee
Out of the foxglove's door,
When butterflies renounce their drams,
I shall but drink the more!

Till seraphs swing their snowy hats,
And saints to windows run,
To see the little tippler
Leaning against the sun!

Another poet who could experience tremendous joy in nature and pass it along to others was Edna St. Vincent Millay. How can one stay mournful in the presence of "God's World."

O world, I can not hold thee close enough!
Thy winds, thy wide grey skies!
Thy mists, that roll and rise!
Thy woods, this autumn Day, that ache and sag
And all but cry with color! That gaunt crag
To crush! To lift the lean of that black bluff!
World, World, I cannot get thee close enough!

Long have I known a glory in it all,
But never knew I this:
Here such a passion is
As stretcheth me apart—Lord I do fear
Thou'st made the world too beautiful this year;
My soul is all but out of me—let fall
No burning leaf; prithee, let no bird call.

Add one capsule of "Afternoon on a Hill," also by Millay:

I will be the gladdest thing
Under the sun!
I will touch a hundred flowers
And not pick one.

I will look at cliffs and clouds
With quiet eyes,
Watch the wind bow down the grass,
And the grass rise.

And when lights begin to show
Up from the town,
I will mark which must be mine,
And then start down!

One of the great sustainers of joy, through his utterly charming
and ridiculous verse was Ogden Nash. Try "A Drink with Something in It" when you've captured the feeling of lightness and joy
and need a handle to hold on to it.

There is something about a Martini,
A tingle remarkably pleasant;

A yellow, a mellow Martini;
I wish that I had one at present.
There is something about a Martini,
Ere the dining and dancing begin,
And to tell you the truth,
It is not the vermouth—
I think that perhaps it's the gin.

There is something about an old-fashioned
That kindles a cardiac glow;
It is soothing and soft and impassioned
As a lyric by Swinburne or Poe.
There is something about an old-fashioned
When dusk has enveloped the sky,
And it may be the ice,
Or the pineapple slice,
But I strongly suspect it's the rye.

There is something about a mint julep,
It is nectar imbibed in a dream,
As fresh as the bud of the tulip,
As cool as the bed of the stream.
There is something about a mint julep,
A fragrance beloved by the lucky.
And perhaps it's the tint
Of the frost and the mint,
But I think it was born in Kentucky.

There is something they put in a highball
That awakens the torpidest brain,
That kindles a spark in the eyeball,
Gliding singing through vein after vein.
There is something they put in a highball
Which you'll notice one day, if you watch;
And it may be the soda,
But judged by the odor,
I rather believe it's the scotch.

Then here's to the heartening wassail,
Wherever good fellows are found;
Be its master instead of its vassal,

And order the glasses around.
For there's something they put in the wassail
That prevents it from tasting like wicker;
Since it's not tapioca,
Or mustard, or mocha,
I'm forced to conclude it's the liquor.

Having been insisting all along that you can't overdose with poem prescriptions, I was shocked to find in my reading that according to Oliver Wendell Holmes, you certainly can. Assuming his verse won't have the effect he claims for it, I include a prescription for sustaining joy that tells of the problems of being *too* joyful. It's called "The Height of the Ridiculous."

I wrote some lines once on a time
In wondrous merry mood,
And thought, as usual, men would say
They were exceeding good.

They were so queer, so very queer,
I laughed as I would die;
Albeit, in the general way,
A sober man am I.

I called my servant, and he came;
How kind it was of him
To mind a slender man like me,
He of the mighty limb!

"These to the printer," I exclaimed,
And, in my humorous way,
I added (as a trifling jest),
"There'll be the devil to pay."

He took the paper, and I watched,
And saw him peep within;
At the first line he read, his face
Was all upon the grin.

He read the next; the grin grew broad,
And shot from ear to ear;

He read the third; a chuckling noise
I now began to hear.

The fourth; he broke into a roar;
The fifth; his waistband split;
The sixth; he burst five buttons off,
And tumbled in a fit.

Ten days and nights, with sleepless eye,
I watched that wretched man,
And since, I never dare to write
As funny as I can.

The following are two small capsules of my own:

The erudite of literature
Have often tried to claim
That Shakespeare didn't write the things
We credit to his name.

In Bartlett's book of famous quotes
The clever clue is hid.
What Shakespeare didn't write himself
It's clear the Ibid did!

And:

It isn't government that rules,
Nor ideologies, nor schools.
The establishment's a social myth
To frighten little children with!

It's obvious, if one observes
The multi-mini-skirted curves,
The bearded chins and owl-eyed glasses,
That fashion is what rules the masses!

It's healthy to poke fun and laugh at the burdens of the world.
We take social and political happenings so seriously, we get up-
tight about them and thereby destroy a large measure of joy. It's
impossible to put out of mind some of the real problems of society,

Poetry for Peace of Mind

but we can avoid wallowing in concern and annoyance at things that are really not disturbing, like long hair, short skirts, and whether Shakespeare really wrote his own plays. The more we can look on the world and ourselves and laugh, the better we and the world will be. Even sorrow and sin have their light side. Try a prescription by Edna St. Vincent Millay called "The Penitent" as a last dose of joy.

> I had a little sorrow,
> Born of a little sin;
> I found a room all damp with gloom
> And shut us all within;
> And, "Little Sorrow, weep," said I,
> "And, Little Sin, pray God to die,
> And I upon the floor will lie
> And think how bad I've been!"
>
> Alas for pious planning—
> It mattered not a whit!
> As far as gloom went in that room
> The lamp might have been lit!
> My Little Sorrow would not weep,
> My Little Sin would go to sleep—
> To save my soul I could not keep
> My graceless mind on it!
>
> So up I got in anger
> And took a book I had,
> And put a ribbon on my hair
> To please a passing lad,
> And, "One thing there's no getting by—
> I've been a wicked girl," said I;
> "But if I can't be sorry, why,
> I might as well be glad!"

X
Fear

Don't confuse fear and anxiety. They are related, but they are really two different things. Anxiety is a nagging nameless unpleasantness. It wraps your body in nerve endings. You almost feel inflamed with it. It comes from nowhere and usually leaves as unpredictably as it came. Fear is something else. Fear is a sudden rush of adrenalin when you find yourself on a railroad track with a train coming. Fear is what you feel when you see a hungry tiger a little too close for comfort.

Fear has an immediately identifiable source. To most of us who don't roam jungles and railroad tracks, fear comes from the illness of a loved one, the loss of a job, the discovery that you have no money and the terrifying reality that you have no source of income. Fear is the moment your brakes fail in the car and you're going down a hill headed for something large and immovable. Obviously, none of these occasions are the right ones for pursuing poetry. Poem prescriptions help only when the fear is prolonged. Poem prescriptions can also serve therapeutically after a crisis, such as an automobile accident, when the nerves are still standing straight up and stinging.

We can't do without fear. It gives us added strength at the moment that it strikes, and it serves as a very constructive warning device. Without it, you might stay on the railroad track and make quiet bets with yourself whether or not the train will hit you. We need fear. But we also need to deal with it so that we won't go

under. One of the best poem prescriptions for rational fear is by
Emily Dickinson.

A narrow fellow in the grass
Occasionally rides;
You may have met him—did you not?
His notice sudden is.

The grass divides as with a comb.
A spotted shaft is seen;
And then it closes at your feet
And opens further on.

He likes a boggy acre,
A floor too cool for corn,
Yet when a child, and barefoot,
I more than once, at morn,

Have passed, I thought, a whip-lash
Unbraiding in the sun,—
When, stooping to secure it,
It wrinkled and was gone.

Several of Nature's people
I know, and they know me;
I feel for them a transport
Of cordiality;

But never met this fellow,
Attended or alone,
Without a tighter breathing,
And zero at the bone.

Snakes are often responsible for a very reasonable fear. We
usually don't know enough about them to trust any of them. Of the
fourteen species indigenous to the northeastern United States, only
two, the copperhead and the timber rattler, are poisonous. Along
with poem prescriptions, read a good book about snakes indigenous
to your area and study it. Learn what to fear and what not to fear.
Use sensible precaution when walking in the woods, and if you're
climbing rocky areas, don't put your hand down without first look-

ing to see where you are putting it. I completely lost my fear of snakes when I met a herpetologist who showed me how to identify them and how to handle them. Snakes are very attractive, friendly, and not unpleasant pets. They are not hostile and have more fear of people than people have of them.

Herman Melville has a prescription for other similar and genuine fears in his poem "The Ribs and Terrors."

The ribs and terrors in the whale,
Arched over me a dismal gloom,
While all God's sun-lit waves rolled by,
And left me deepening down to doom.

I saw the opening maw of hell,
With endless pains and sorrows there;
Which none but they that feel can tell—
Oh, I was plunging to despair.

In black distress, I called my God,
When I could scarce believe him mine,
He bowed his ear to my complaints—
No more the whale did me confine.

With speed he flew to my relief,
As on a radiant dolphin borne;
Awful, yet bright, as lightning shone
The face of my Deliverer God.

My song forever shall record
That terrible, that joyful hour;
I give the glory to my God,
His all the mercy and the power.

The fear of growing old is very real because it is going to happen. With age comes the fear of losing faculties, concern about where and how we will live—perhaps on a very limited income. Because of its inevitability, we can only learn to live with the foreknowledge of age and accept it. Poems help to instill the wisdom age needs and they serve therapeutically in dealing with oncoming time. Some people age magnificently. I know several who have carried their alertness, agility, involvements, and humor into their eighties and nineties. In studying the character and conditions of elderly people, it becomes apparent that the secret of alert longevity is in the attitude of mind with which one moves down the corridor of time. Dr. Tehyi Hsieh, a Chinese diplomat and justice of the peace in Brighton, Massachusetts, lived all his ninety-one years with incredible vigor. His days were spent working and performing his duties as justice of the peace. He married a thousand couples each year, wrote three books, and continued to travel until he was ninety from Boston as far as Canada to lecture on the differences and problems between the two Chinas he knew so well.

Morris Ernst, famous trial lawyer and author of more than thirty books, was still busily engaged in legal affairs past the age of eighty. He continued to appear at his law office every day and carried on the professional and social life he'd always enjoyed until his death at eighty-seven. Curiously, he claimed that the activity kept him young, and there wasn't a topic or an action in the world that didn't make his mind leap.

John Masefield has a poem prescription for the fear of growing old:

Be with me, Beauty, for the fire is dying;
My dog and I are old, too old for roving.
Man, whose young passion sets the spindrift flying,
Is soon too lame to march, too cold for loving.
I take the book and gather to the fire,
Turning old yellow leaves; minute by minute
The clock ticks to my heart. A withered wire,
Moves a thin ghost of music in the spinet.
I cannot sail your seas, I cannot wander
Your cornland, nor your hill-land, nor your valleys
Ever again, nor share the battle yonder
Where the young knight the broken squadron rallies.
Only stay quiet while my mind remembers
The beauty of fires from the beauty of embers.

Beauty, have pity! for the strong have power,
The rich their wealth, the beautiful their grace,
Summer of man is sunlight and its flower,
Spring-time of man all April in a face.

Only, as in the jostling in the Strand,
Where the mob thrusts or loiters or is loud,
The beggar with the saucer in his hand
Asks only a penny from the passing crowd,
So, from this glittering world with all its fashion,
Its fire, and play of men, its stir, its march,
Let me have wisdom, Beauty, wisdom and passion,
Bread to the soul, rain when the summers parch.
Give me but these, and though the darkness close
Even the night will blossom as the rose.

Often part of the fear of aging is the fear of death, but why shouldn't death be as beautiful as birth! Joseph Blanco White wrote the next prescription for fear in his poem "To Night."

Mysterious Night! when our first parent knew
Thee from report divine, and heard thy name,
Did he not tremble for this lovely frame,
This glorious canopy of light and blue?
Yet 'neath a curtain of translucent dew,
Bathed in the rays of the great setting flame,
Hesperus with the host of heaven came,
And lo! Creation widened on man's view.
Who could have thought such darkness lay concealed
Within thy beams, O Sun! or who could find,
Whilst fly and leaf and insect stood revealed,
That to such countless orbs thou mad'st us blind!
Why do we then shun death with anxious strife?
If Light can thus deceive, wherefore not Life?

In the same vein, Walter Savage Landor's, "Leaf After Leaf."

Leaf after leaf drops off, flower after flower,
Some in the chill, some in the warmer hour:
Alike they flourish and alike they fall,
And earth who nourished them receives them all.
Should we, her wiser sons, be less content
To sink into her lap when life is spent?

In many areas today there are real reasons to fear who you might find in your house as an uninvited guest. Robert Frost's "House Fear" has the power to allay this concern; it's so reasonable.

Always—I tell you this they learned—
Always at night when they returned
To the lonely house from far away
To lamps unlighted and the fire gone gray,
They learned to rattle the lock and key
To give whatever might chance to be
Warning and time to be off in flight!
And preferring the out- to the in-door night,
They learned to leave the house door wide
Until they had lit the lamp inside.

Storms are another reasonable cause for fear. They *do* do damage. Robert Frost also wrote the next prescription, "Storm Fear."

When the wind works against us in the dark,
And pelts with snow
The lower chamber window on the east,
And whispers with a sort of stifled bark,
The beast,
"Come out! Come out!"
It costs no inward struggle not to go,
Ah, no!
I count our strength,
Two and a child,
Those of us not asleep subdued to mark
How the cold creeps as the fire dies at length,—
How drifts are piled,
Dooryard and road ungraded,
Till even the comforting barn grows far away,
And my heart owns a doubt
Whether 'tis in us to arise with day
And save ourselves unaided.

Phyllis McGinley wrote the next prescription for fear. It's called, "Mid Century Love Letter," but it has comforting tones and rhythms applicable to any fear.

Stay near me. Speak my name. Oh, do not wander
By the thought's span, heart's impulse, from the light
We kindle here. You are my sole defender
(As I am yours) in this precipitous night,
Which over earth, till common landmarks alter,
Is falling, without stars, and bitter cold.
We two have but our burning selves for shelter.
Huddle against me. Give me your hand to hold.
So might two climbers lost in mountain weather
On a high slope and taken by the storm,
Desperate in the darkness, cling together
Under one cloak and breathe each other warm.
Stay near me. Spirit, perishable as bone,
In no such winter can survive alone.

Fears concerning the world in general, and man's annihilation of himself in particular, can be genuine. "The Nile" is a prescription poem by Leigh Hunt.

It flows through old hushed Egypt and its sands,
Like some grave mighty thought threading a dream,
And times and things, as in that vision, seem
Keeping along it with eternal stands,
Caves, pillars, pyramids, the shepherd bands
That roamed through the young world, the glory extreme
Of high Sesostris, and that southern beam,
Of laughing queen that caught the world's great hands.
Then comes a mightier silence, stern and strong,
As of a world left empty of its throng,
And the void weighs on us; and then we wake,
And hear the fruitful stream lapsing along
'Twixt villages, and think how we shall take
Our own calm journey on for human sake.

No matter how we abuse it, the world shall lapse along and so shall we. Sometimes even the larger despairs of the universe can be looked at lightly. Humor is a ballast for every woe. Following are two small prescriptions of mine for relief from the fear of a few social disorders.

I cannot believe that there's any need
To alter the mind with pot or speed
When women without such drugs as these
Have been doing it now for centuries.

And:

In the city you had dirt and din
And crime and air pollution,
So naturally you and your kin
Thought the suburbs the solution.

Here, peace you figure will prevail
But you find within an hour
A raccoon in the garbage pail
And spiders in the shower.

The next prescription for allaying fear is by A. E. Housman and is called "I to My Perils."

I to my perils
Of cheat and charmer
Come clad in armour
By stars benign;
Hope lies to mortals
And most believe her,
But man's deceiver
Was never mine.

The thoughts of others
Were light and fleeting,
Of lover's meeting
Or luck or fame;
Mine were of trouble
And mine were steady,
So I was ready
When trouble came.

The last prescription is a sonnet by William Wordsworth, who offers it as a solace for any problem of living:

Nuns fret not at their convent's narrow room;
And hermits are contented with their cells;
And students with their pensive citadels;
Maids at the wheel, the weaver at his loom,
Sit blithe and happy; bees that soar for bloom,
High as the highest peak of Furness-fells,
Will murmur by the hour in foxglove bells:
In truth the prison, unto which we doom
Ourselves, no prison is: and hence for me,
In sundry moods, 'twas pastime to be bound
Within the Sonnet's scanty plot of ground;
Pleased if some souls (for such there needs must be)
Who have felt the weight of too much liberty,
Should find brief solace there, as I have found.

Wordsworth knew the healing power in both reading and writing poetry. He also knew that most mortals make their own prisons. What is there to fear when we have locked ourselves up by our own free will and can, if we choose, unlock ourselves again?

XI

To Relieve Boredom

Boredom may be depression in another guise. It doesn't matter what starts it, as long as you can make use of a sure-fire way to shout it down. However, boredom is tenacious. You have to be stronger than it is to make it give in. When boredom strikes, you know it because suddenly you find yourself not really wanting to do anything. Your mind might even run off a list of all the things you could be doing, but because you don't want to do any of them, boredom persists.

There's not much point in telling yourself about the things you haven't done and should be doing. What you want precisely is to be entertained with the least possible effort on your part. Poetry can do this for you. The best poems for pure entertainment are the story poems or ballads—poems that take you somewhere, stir you up, and set your mind on a positive track again. Most of the prescriptions for boredom that I've selected are right out of your past. This makes them even more helpful, because they have the ring of familiarity that makes any good poem better. They also have a chant and beat that moves them along easily. They are surely not obscure or difficult to interpret, so your bored and boggled mind won't rebel. In them, you have drama and rhythm and not too much head work. The next time you are bored, take a dose of "The Landing of the Pilgrims" by Felicia Dorothea Hemans.

> The breaking waves dashed high
> On a stern and rock-bound coast,

And the woods against a stormy sky
Their giant branches tossed;
And the heavy night hung dark
The hills and waters o'er,
When a band of exiles moored their bark
On the wild New England shore.

Not as the conqueror comes,
They, the true-hearted, came;
Not with the roll of the stirring drums,
And the trumpet that sings of fame;
Not as the flying come,
In silence and in fear;
They shook the depths of the desert's gloom
With their hymns of lofty cheer.

Amidst the storm they sang;
And the stars heard, and the sea;
And the sounding aisles of the dim woods rang
To the anthem of the free.
The ocean eagle soared
From his nest by the white wave's foam;
And the rocking pines of the forest roared;
This was their welcome home!

There were men with hoary hair
Amidst that pilgrim band:
Why had they come to wither there,
Away from their childhood's land?
There was woman's fearless eye,
Lit by her deep love's truth;
There was manhood's brow, serenely high,
And the fiery heart of youth.

What sought they thus afar?
Bright jewels of the mine?
The wealth of seas, the spoils of war?—
They sought a faith's pure shrine!
Aye, call it holy ground,
The soil where first they trod;

They have left unstained what there they found—
Freedom to worship God!

The patriotic fervor of "The Landing of the Pilgrims" starts the adrenalin flowing in our system and launches a strong attack against boredom.

There's a listlessness to boredom that the surge and stir of a good story-poem whips about. Science has invented so many "work-savers" that we are driven into boredom more than in any other era and it is harder to combat today. We do not labor as hard physically as our forefathers did, and we certainly have more idle time available. It wasn't always so; boredom is a modern syndrome. The pilgrims didn't whimper about their plight—they were too busy carving a community out of a virgin wilderness.

Neither did the village blacksmith in the days of hand-forged horseshoes. My second poem prescription for boredom is "The Village Blacksmith" by Henry Wadsworth Longfellow. Remember when you had to memorize it and chant it aloud at a school performance?

> Under a spreading chestnut tree
> The village smithy stands;
> The smith, a mighty man is he,
> With large and sinewy hands;
> And the muscles of his brawny arms
> Are strong as iron bands.
>
> His hair is crisp, and black, and long,
> His face is like the tan;
> His brow is wet with honest sweat,
> He earns whate'er he can,
> And looks the whole world in the face,
> For he owes not any man.
>
> Week in, week out, from morn till night,
> You can hear his bellows blow;
> You can hear him swing his heavy sledge,
> With measured beat and slow,
> Like a sexton ringing the village bell,
> When the evening sun is low.

And the children coming home from school
Look in at the open door;
They love to see the flaming forge,
And hear the bellows roar,
And catch the burning sparks that fly
Like chaff from a threshing-floor.

He goes on Sunday to the church,
And sits among his boys;
He hears the parson pray and preach,
He hears his daughter's voice,
Singing in the village choir,
And it makes his heart rejoice.

It sounds to him like her mother's voice,
Singing in Paradise!
He needs must think of her once more,
Now in the grave she lies;
And with his hard, rough hand he wipes
A tear out of his eyes.

Toiling, rejoicing, sorrowing,
Onward through life he goes;
Each morning sees some task begin,
Each evening sees it close;
Something attempted, something done,
Has earned a night's repose.

Thanks, thanks to thee, my worthy friend,
For the lesson thou has taught!
Thus at the flaming forge of life
Our fortunes must be wrought;
Thus on its sounding anvil shaped
Each burning deed and thought.

When boredom descends, we either float about pointlessly, half-looking for something to do, or we crawl off somewhere and brood. Perhaps more than one great poem was conceived in a moody, brooding stillness; but one in particular is a story-poem that a gloom mood brought forth at the end of the nineteenth century from

Thomas Hardy. It's called "The Souls of the Slain"—my next prescription for boredom.

> The thick lids of the night closed upon me
> Alone at the Bill
> Of the isle by the Race—
> Many-caverned, bald, wrinkled of face—
> And with darkness and silence the spirit was on me
> To brood and be still.
>
> No wind fanned the flats of the ocean,
> Or promontory sides,
> Or the ooze by the strand,
> Or the bent-bearded slope of the land,
> Whose base took its rest amid everlong motion
> Of criss-crossing tides.
>
> Soon from out of the southward seemed nearing
> A whirr, as of wings
> Waved by mighty-vanned flies,
> Or by night-moths of measureless size,
> And in softness and smoothness well-nigh beyond hearing
> Of corporal things.
>
> And they bore to the bluff, and alighted—
> A dim-discerned train
> Of sprites without mould,
> Frameless souls none might touch or might hold—
> On the ledge by the turreted lantern, far-sighted
> By men of the main.
>
> And I heard them say "Home!" and I knew them
> For souls of the felled
> On the earth's nether bord
> Under Capricorn, whither they'd warred,
> And I neared in my awe, and gave heedfulness to them
> With breathings inheld.
>
> Then it seemed there approached from the northward
> A senior soul-flame
> Of the like filmy hue;

And he met them and spake: "Is it you,
O my men?" Said they, "Aye! We bear homeward and
hearthward
To feast on our fame!"

"I've flown there before you," he said then:
"Your households are well;
But—your kin linger less
On your glory and war-mightiness
Than on dearer things,"—"Dearer?" cried these from the dead
then,
"Of what do they tell?"

"Some mothers muse sadly, and murmur
Your doings as boys—
Recall the quaint ways
Of your babyhood's innocent days.
Some pray that, ere dying, your faith had grown firmer,
And higher your joys.

"A father broods: 'Would I had set him
To some humble trade,
And so slacked his high fire,
And his passionate martial desire;
And told him no stories to woo him and whet him
To this dire crusade!'"

"And, General, how hold out our sweethearts,
Sworn loyal as doves?"
—"Many mourn; many think
It is not unattractive to prink
Them in sables for heros. Some fickle and fleet hearts
Have found them new loves."

"And our wives?" quoth another resignedly,
"Dwell they on our deeds?"
—"Deeds of home; that live yet
Fresh as new—deeds of fondness or fret;
Ancient words that were kindly expressed or unkindly,
These, these have their heeds."

—"Alas! then it seems that our glory
Weighs less in their thought
Than our old homely acts,
And the long-ago commonplace facts
Of our lives—held by us as scarce part of our story,
And rated as nought!"

Then bitterly some: "Was it wise now
To raise the tomb-door
For such knowledge? Away!"
But the rest: "Fame we prized till to-day;
Yet that hearts keep us green for old kindness we prize now
A thousand times more!"

Thus speaking, the trooped apparitions
Began to disband
And resolve them in two:
Those whose record was lovely and true
Bore to northward for home: Those of bitter traditions
Again left the land,

And, towering to seaward in legions,
They paused at a spot
Overbending the Race—
That engulphing, ghast, sinister place—
Whither headlong they plunged, to the fathomless regions
Of myriads forgot.

And the spirits of those who were homing
Passed on rushingly,
Like the Pentecost Wind;
And the whirr of their wayfaring thinned
And surceased on the sky, and but left in the gloaming
Sea-mutterings and me.

A great many fine ballads came from out of the wars. For some
reason, the sound and beat and roll of battle relates to the rhythm
of poetry. There are hoofbeats, drumbeats, and the drama and
intensity of trying to stay alive. It's frightening to consider how
many men have loved war and recall their part in it as the greatest

part they ever played. For many, World War II held their finest hours. Wasteful and horrible as war is, there is much to be said for the honors won and the glory incurred while fighting a noble and honorable cause. I met a man in England in 1964 who had flown the Mosquito bombers in the Second World War. He reveled in recalling the war and his near-fatal encounters. It was the high spot of his whole existence. While it has not been found to be the answer to the troubles of nations, some magnificent behavior has emerged under fire; many men have found a new kind of humanness in their comrades and have attributed characteristics that group them with the gods. Such a man was Rudyard Kipling's "Gunga Din."

You may talk o' gin and beer
When you're quartered safe out 'ere,
An' you're sent to penny-fights an' Aldershot it;
But when it comes to slaughter
You will do your work on water,
An' you'll lick the bloomin' boots of 'im that's got it.
Now in Injia's sunny clime,
Where I used to spend my time
A-servin' of 'Er Majesty the Queen,
Of all them black-faced crew
The finest man I knew
Was our regimental bhisti, Gunga Din.

He was "Din! Din! Din!
You limpin' lump o' brick-dust, Gunga Din!
Hi! *slippey hitherao!*
Water! get it! *Panee lao!*
You squidgy-nosed old idol, Gunga Din!"

The uniform 'e wore
Was nothin' much before,
An' rather less than 'arf o' that be'ind,
For a piece o' twisty rag
An' a goatskin water-bag
Was all the field-equipment 'e could find.
When the sweatin' troop-train lay
In a sidin' through the day,

Where the 'eat would make your bloomin' eye-brows crawl,
We shouted "Harry By!"
Till our throats were bricky-dry,
Then we wopped 'im 'cause 'e couldn't serve us all.

It was "Din! Din! Din!
You 'eathen, where the mischief 'ave you been?
You put some *juldee* in it
Or I'll *marrow* you this minute,
If you don't fill up my helmet, Gunga Din!"

'E would dot an' carry one
Till the longest day was done;
An' 'e didn't seem to know the use o' fear.
If we charged or broke or cut,
You could bet your bloomin' nut,
'E'd be waitin' fifty paces right flank rear.
With 'is mussick on 'is back,
'E would skip with our attack,
An' watch us till the bugles made "Retire,"
An' for all 'is dirty 'ide
'E was white, clear white, inside
When 'e went to tend the wounded under fire!

It was "Din! Din! Din!"
With the bullets kicking dust-spots on the green
When the cartridges ran out,
You could hear the front-files shout,
"Hi! ammunition-mules an' Gunga Din!"

I sha'n't forgit the night
When I dropped be'ind the fight
With a bullet where my belt-plate should 'a' been.
I was chokin' mad with thirst,
An' the man that spied me first
Was our good old grinnin', gruntin' Gunga Din.
'E lifted up my 'ead,
An' 'e plugged me where I bled,
An' 'e guv me 'arf-a-pint o' water—green:
It was crawlin' an' it stunk,
But of all the drinks I've drunk,
I'm gratefullest to one from Gunga Din.

It was "Din! Din! Din!
'Ere's a beggar with a bullet through 'is spleen;
'E's chawin' up the ground,
An' 'e's kickin' all around:
For Gawd's sake git the water, Gunga Din."

'E carried me away
To where a *dooli* lay,
An' a bullet came an' drilled the beggar clean.
'E put me safe inside,
An' just before 'e died:
"I 'ope you liked your drink," sez Gunga Din.
So I'll meet him later on
At the place where 'e is gone—
Where it's always double drill an' no canteen;
'E'll be squattin' on the coals,
Given' drink to pore damned souls,
An' I'll git a swig in hell from Gunga Din!

Yes, Din! Din! Din!
You Lazarushian-leather Gunga Din!
Though I've belted you an' flayed you,
By the livin' Gawd that made you,
You're a better man than I am, Gunga Din!

It's sad that there have been men who needed the drama of war
to hold back the dregs of boredom, and who have found civilian
life drab and uninteresting and bleak. Boredom has to be fought
like a battle and it shouldn't be hard, for we do, after all, create it.
It's a condition of mind that we have allowed to happen in a
world filled with a million undone things and another million
miracles yet to be born.

My next prescription for boredom is from Sir Walter Scott in
the days of damsels and bright balls and dashing young horsemen
who fought for their loves against the barricades of parental objec-
tions. Boredom will disappear quickly with the reading of "Lochinvar."

Oh, young Lochinvar is come out of the west;
Through all the wide Border his steed was the best;

Poetry for Peace of Mind

And save his good broadsword he weapons had none;
He rode all unarmed, and he rode all alone.
So faithful in love, and so dauntless in war,
There never was knight like the young Lochinvar.

He stayed not for brake, and he stopped not for stone;
He swam the Eske river where ford there was none;
But ere he alighted at Netherby gate,
The bride had consented, the gallant came late:
For a laggard in love, and a dastard in war,
Was to wed the fair Ellen of brave Lochinvar.

So boldly he entered the Netherby hall,
Among bridesmen and kinsmen, and brothers and all.
Then spoke the bride's father, his hand on his sword
(for the poor craven bridegroom said never a word),
"Oh, come ye in peace here, or come you in war,
Or to dance at our bridal, young Lord Lochinvar?"

"I long wooed your daughter, my suit you denied.
Love swells like the Solway, but ebbs like its tide;
And now I am come, with this lost love of mine
To lead but one measure, drink one cup of wine.
There are maidens in Scotland more lovely by far
That would gladly be bride to the young Lochinvar."

The bride kissed the goblet; the knight took it up:
He quaffed off the wine, and he threw down the cup.
She looked down to blush, and she looked up to sigh,
With a smile on her lips and a tear in her eye.
He took her soft hand ere her mother could bar,—
"Now tread we a measure!" said young Lochinvar.

So stately his form, and so lovely her face,
That never a hall such a galliard did grace;
While her mother did fret, and her father did fume,
And the bridegroom stood dangling his bonnet and plume;
And the bridemaidens whispered, " 'Twere better by far
To have matched our fair cousin with young Lochinvar."

One touch to her hand, and one word in her ear,
When they reached the hall door and the charger stood near;

So light to the croupe the fair lady he swung,
So light to the saddle before her he sprung!
"She is won! we are gone, over bank, bush, and scaur!
They'll have fleet steeds that follow!" quoth young Lochinvar.

There was mounting 'mong Graemes of the Netherby clan;
Forsters, Fenwicks, and Musgraves, they rode and they ran;
There was racing and chasing on Cannobie Lee;
But the lost bride of Netherby ne'er did they see.
So daring in love, and so dauntless in war,
Have ye e'er heard of gallant like young Lochinvar?

If boredom still plagues you, take a dose of "Barbara Frietchie" by John Greenleaf Whittier.

Up from the meadows rich with corn,
Clear in the cool September morn,

The clustered spires of Frederick stand,
Green-walled by the hills of Maryland.

Round about them orchards sweep,
Apple and peach tree fruited deep,

Fair as a garden of the Lord
To the eyes of the famished rebel horde,

On that pleasant morn of the early fall
When Lee marched over the mountain wall,—

Over the mountains, winding down,
Horse and foot, into Frederick town.

Forty flags with their silver stars,
Forty flags with their crimson bars,

Flapped in the morning wind; the sun
Of noon looked down, and saw not one.

Up rose old Barbara Frietchie then,
Bowed with her fourscore years and ten;

Bravest of all in Frederick town,
She took up the flag the men hauled down;

In her attic window the staff she set,
To show that one heart was loyal yet.

Up the street came the rebel tread,
Stonewall Jackson riding ahead.

Under his slouched hat left and right
He glanced: the old flag met his sight.

"Halt!"—the dust-brown ranks stood fast;
"Fire!"—out blazed the rifle-blast.

It shivered the window, pane and sash;
It rent the banner with seam and gash.

Quick, as it fell, from the broken staff
Dame Barbara snatched the silken scarf;

She leaned far out on the window-sill,
And shook it forth with a royal will.

"Shoot, if you must, this old gray head,
But spare your country's flag," she said.

A shade of sadness, a blush of shame,
Over the face of the leader came;

The nobler nature within him stirred
To life at that woman's deed and word:

"Who touches a hair of yon gray head
Dies like a dog! March on!" he said.

All day long through Frederick street
Sounded the tread of marching feet;

All day long that free flag tost
Over the heads of the rebel host.

Ever its torn folds rose and fell
On the loyal winds that loved it well;

And through the hill-gaps sunset light
Shone over it with a warm good-night.

Barbara Frietchie's work is o'er,
And the rebel rides on his raids no more.

Honor to her! and let a tear
Fall, for her sake, on Stonewall's bier.

Over Barbara Frietchie's grave,
Flag of freedom and union, wave!

Peace and order and beauty draw
Round thy symbol of light and law;

And ever the stars above look down
On thy stars below in Frederick town.

The last prescription for boredom isn't a ballad or story poem, exactly. Nor does it concern itself with war and history as so many poems do. It's a brief autobiography of a woman who never knew a moment's boredom in her life and who knew the reason why. It's a good capsule to take for the discomfort of a bored mind. Meet "Lucinda Matlock" by Edgar Lee Masters:

I went to the dances at Chandlerville,
And played snap-out at Winchester.
One time we exchanged partners,
Driving home in the moonlight of a middle June,
And then I found Davis.
We were married and lived together for seventy years,
Enjoying, working, raising the twelve children,
Eight of whom we lost
Ere I had reached the age of sixty.
I spun, I wove, I kept the house, I nursed the sick,
I made the garden, and for holiday
Rambled over the fields where sang the larks,
And by Spoon River gathering many a shell,
And many a flower and medicinal weed—
Shouting to the wooden hills, singing to the green valleys.
At ninety-six I had lived enough, that is all,
And passed to a sweet repose.
What is this I hear of sorrow and weariness,
Anger, discontent and drooping hopes?
Degenerate sons and daughters,
Life is too strong for you—
It takes life to love life.

XII
Fatigue

Fatigue is a complaint that only rest will cure, but in the frenetic pace of modern living, the ability to rest needs to be learned. It's one thing to place the body in a comfortable position and wait for rest to happen. It's quite another to slow down the mind so it can. Fatigue usually occurs at the end of day, most often in the late afternoon when the blood sugar is low and the day's demands have used up stored energies. Many people get a second wind after dinner and go on to further work or entertainment. Others continue to be fatigued and do very little until bedtime.

The poem prescriptions that I have selected for fatigue should be taken about five o'clock in the afternoon. During most of the year (except for those living in the land of the midnight sun) this is the time of twilight. The birds change their songs to subtle tunes, winds die down, and, as Thomas Hardy says, "Most men have sought their household fires." It's a time for reflection and peaceful unwinding. For many it's teatime, and for others it's the cocktail hour. For everyone it should be a quiet hour for rest and the mental ingestion of poetry to stir the memory of good things past. You might start with a small dose called "Sweet Was the Song" by Walter Savage Landor.

> Sweet was the song that Youth sang once,
> And passing sweet was the response;
> But there are accents sweeter far

When love leaps down our evening star,
Holds back the blighting wings of time,
Melts with his breath the crusty rime,
And looks into our eyes and says,
"Come, let us talk of former days."

Poem prescriptions can help you recall moments of peaceful happiness, and as your mind is soothed, so are your muscles. Thomas Love Peacock's "Love and Age" is a reflective look at a long life and an old love. Perhaps it will stir a similar memory in you.

I played with you 'mid cowslips blowing,
When I was six and you were four;
When garlands weaving, flower-balls throwing,
Were pleasures soon to please no more.
Through groves and meads, o'er grass and heather,
With little playmates, to and fro,
We wandered hand in hand together;
But that was sixty years ago.

You grew a lovely roseate maiden,
And still our early love was strong;
Still with no care our days were laden,
They glided joyously along;
Then I did love you, very dearly,
How dearly words want power to show;
I thought your heart was touched as nearly;
But that was fifty years ago.

Then other lovers came around you,
Your beauty grew from year to year,
And many a splendid circle found you
The center of its glittering sphere.
I saw you then, first vows forsaking,
On rank and wealth your hand bestow;
Oh, then I thought my heart was breaking,—
But that was forty years ago.

And I lived on, to wed another:
No cause she gave me to repine;

And when I heard you were a mother,
I did not wish the children mine.
My own young flock, in fair progression,
Made up a pleasant Christmas row:
My joy in them was past expression;—
But that was thirty years ago.

You grew a matron plump and comely,
You dwelt in fashion's brightest blaze:
My earthly lot was far more homely;
But I too had my festal days.
No merrier eyes have ever glistened
Around the hearth-stone's wintry glow,
Than when my youngest child was christened:—
But that was twenty years ago.

Time passed. My eldest girl was married,
And I am now a grandsire grey;
One pet of four years old I've carried
Among the wild-flowered meads to play.
In our old fields of childish pleasure,
Where now, as then, the cowslips blow,
She fills her basket's ample measure,—
And that is not ten years ago.

But though first love's impassioned blindness
Has passed away in colder light,
I still have thought of you with kindness,
And shall do, till our last good-night.
The ever-rolling silent hours
Will bring a time we shall not know,
When our young days of gathering flowers
Will be an hundred years ago.

Fatigue comes from physical or mental hard work, and as in all physical and mental complaints the safest, sanest cure is to touch base with nature. Earth, water, sky, trees, and clouds contain the truest, purest secrets for survival. Here is a prescription for that weary feeling. Take it at twilight, preferably settled in a large easy chair. "The Cloud" by Percy Bysshe Shelley:

I bring fresh showers for the thirsting flowers,
From the seas and the streams;
I bear light shade for the leaves when laid
In their noonday dreams.
From my wings are shaken the dews that waken
The sweet buds every one,
When rocked to rest on their mother's breast,
As she dances about the sun.
I wield the flail of the lashing hail,
And whiten the green plains under,
And then again I dissolve it in rain,
And laugh as I pass in thunder.

I sift the snow on the mountains below,
And their great pines groan aghast;
And all the night 'tis my pillow white,
While I sleep in the arms of the blast.
Sublime on the towers of my skiey bowers,
Lightning my pilot sits;
In a cavern under is fettered the thunder,
It struggles and howls at fits;
Over earth and ocean, with gentle motion,
This pilot is guiding me,
Lured by the love of the genii that move
In the depths of the purple sea;
Over the rills, and the crags, and the hills,
Over the lakes and the plains,
Wherever he dream, under mountain or stream,
The spirit he loves remains;
And I all the while bask in heaven's blue smile,
Whilst he is dissolving in rains.

The sanguine sunrise, with his meteor eyes,
And his burning plumes outspread,
Leaps on the back of my sailing rack,
When the morning star shines dead;
As on the jag of a mountain crag,
Which an earthquake rocks and swings,
An eagle alit one moment may sit
In the light of its golden wings.

And when sunset may breathe, from the lit sea beneath,
Its ardours of rest and of love,
And the crimson pall of eve may fall
From the depths of heaven above,
With wings folded I rest, on mine aery nest,
As still as a brooding dove.

That orbed Maiden with white fire laden,
Whom mortals call the moon,
Glides glimmering o'er my fleece-like floor,
By the mid-night breezes strewn;
And whenever the beat of her unseen feet,
Which only the angels hear,
May have broken the woof of my tent's thin roof,
The stars peep behind her and peer;
And I laugh to see them whirl and flee,
Like a swarm of golden bees,
When I widen the rent in my wind-built tent,
Till the calm rivers, lakes, and seas,
Like strips of the sky fallen through me on high,
Are each paved with the moon and these.

I bind the earth's throne with a burning zone,
And the moon's with a girdle of pearl;
The volcanoes are dim, and the stars reel and swim,
When the whirlwinds my banner unfurl.
From cape to cape, with a bridge-like shape,
Over a torrent sea,
Sunbeam-proof, I hang like a roof,—
The mountains its columns be.
The triumphal arch through which I march
With hurricane, fire, and snow,
When the powers of the air are chained to my chair,
Is the million-colored bow;
The sphere-fire above its soft colors wove,
While the moist earth was laughing below.

I am the daughter of Earth and Water,
And the nursling of the Sky,
I pass through the pores of the ocean and shores;

I change, but I cannot die.
For after the rain when with never a stain
The Pavilion of Heaven is bare,
And the winds and sunbeams with their convex gleams
Build up the blue dome of air,
I silently laugh at my own cenotaph,
And out of the caverns of rain,
Like a child from the womb, like a ghost from the tomb,
I arise and unbuild it again.

Body fatigue brings with it a weariness of mind. The two central forces that make up our being are closely interrelated. The long trek home at the end of the day is sweet, although harder to make than the morning trip. Home beckons with an appeal it may not have at any other time. Home is the place for building castles and dreams, and the end of the day is the time for fire-hugging and corner sitting. Take a big dose of Robert Frost's "The Kitchen Chimney" when fatigue overtakes you.

Builder, in building the little house,
In every way you may please yourself;
But please please me in the kitchen chimney:
Don't build me a chimney upon a shelf.

However far you may go for bricks,
Whatever they cost a-piece or a pound,
Buy me enough for a full-length chimney,
And build the chimney clear from the ground.

It's not that I'm greatly afraid of fire,
But I never heard of a house that throve
(And I know of one that didn't thrive)
Where the chimney started above the stove.

And I dread the ominous stain of tar
That there always is on the papered walls,
And the smell of fire drowned in rain
That there always is when the chimney's false.

A shelf's for a clock or vase or picture
But I don't see why it should have to bear

A chimney that only would serve to remind me
Of castles I used to build in air.

Times of fatigue and firesides are times for the soft contemplation of love. To the very tired, love is a balm. When you are worn-out and weary, try these prescriptions. First, a sonnet by Elizabeth Barrett Browning:

How do I love thee? Let me count the ways.
I love thee to the depth and breadth and height
My soul can reach, when feeling out of sight
For the ends of Being and ideal Grace.
Most quiet need, by sun and candle-light,
I love thee freely, as men strive for Right;
I love thee purely, as they turn from Praise.
I love thee with the passion put to use
In my old griefs, and with my childhood's faith.
I love thee with a love I seemed to lose
With my lost saints—I love thee with the breath,
Smiles, tears, of all my life!—and if God choose,
I shall but love thee better after death.

Second, "When You Are Old" by William Butler Yeats:

When you are old and grey and full of sleep,
And nodding by the fire, take down this book,
And slowly read, and dream of the soft look
Your eyes had once, and of their shadows deep;

How many loved your moments of glad grace,
And loved your beauty with false love or true,
But one man loved the pilgrim soul in you,
And loved the sorrows of your changing face;

And bending down beside the glowing bars,
Murmur, a little sadly, how Love fled
And paced upon the mountains overhead
And his face amid a crowd of stars.

And third, a sonnet by William Shakespeare:

> Shall I compare thee to a summer's day?
> Thou art more lovely and more temperate:
> Rough winds do shake the darling buds of May,
> And summer's lease hath all too short a date:
> Sometimes too hot the eye of heaven shines,
> And often is his gold complexion dimm'd;
> And every fair from fair sometimes declines,
> By chance or nature's changing course untrimm'd:
> But thy eternal summer shall not fade
> Nor lose possession of that fair thou owest;
> Nor shall death brag thou wanderest in his shade,
> When in eternal lines to time thou growest;
> So long as men can breathe, or eyes can see,
> So long lives this, and this gives life to thee.

Now, in your chair by the fire, recall some moment of mild triumph. Something that called on your energies and rewarded you with accomplishment. To help you find it is a prescription for fatigue from John Betjeman called "Seaside Golf."

> How straight it flew, how long it flew,
> It cleared the rutty track
> And soaring, disappeared from view
> Beyond the bunker's back—
> A glorious, sailing, bounding drive
> That made me glad I was alive.
>
> And down the fairway, far along
> It glowed a lonely white;
> I played an iron sure and strong
> And clipp'd it out of sight,
> And spite of grassy banks between
> I knew I'd find it on the green.
>
> And so I did. It lay content
> Two paces from the pin;
> A steady putt and then it went
> Oh, most securely in.

The very turf rejoiced to see
The quite unprecedented three.

Ah! Seaweed smells from sandy caves
And thyme and mist in whiffs,
In-coming tide, Atlantic waves
Slapping the sunny cliffs,
Lark song and sea sounds in the air
And splendour, splendour everywhere.

Richard Wilbur has written a sonnet that is a beautiful prescription to relieve fatigue. In this poem, you receive some of the satisfaction that comes with many good jobs well done. At these times, fatigue is a welcome complaint. It's good to feel tired when you have accomplished some worthwhile task.

The winter deepening, the hay all in,
The barn fat with cattle, the apple-crop
Conveyed to market or the fragrant bin,
He thinks the time has come to make a stop,

And sinks half-grudging in his firelit seat,
Though with his heavy body's full consent,
In what would be the posture of defeat,
But for that look of rigorous content.

Outside, the night dives down like one great crow
Against his cast-off clothing where it stands
Up to the knees in miles of hustled snow,

Flapping and jumping like a kind of fire,
And floating skyward its abandoned hands
In gestures of invincible desire.

My last prescription for fatigue is from my own collection of verse. It's called "Evening."

So many times she'd called him in at dusk,
And he recalled the spectered voice on air
That floated to him, house-drawn, in the dim,
Remembered valley that was prisoned there.

She'd held his unity to discipline,
And, bodiless, infused the summer night
With calling sounds that carried to his ears
The mild restrictions of a mother's might.

Reluctant in the shadows he would part
With all the early summer dusk contains
And follow down the valley of her voice
Homeward through the dim, devouring lanes,

Across the years, now filled with summers gone,
He'd trailed her homeward, and without defense.
Summer cupped upward to a mountain held
Within the valley of obedience.

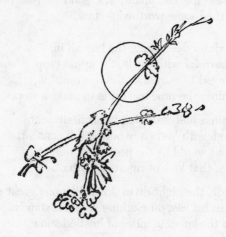

Poetry for Peace of Mind

XIII
Dependency

Caroline, whose voice was the voice of a little girl, was thirty-eight when I first met her. She had been a patient at Pilgrim State Hospital for nearly ten years. She was so dependent upon her parents that she could only function in the womblike security of the institution. She began to show more and more independence after working with poetry therapy. The poem that helped her the most was one from *The Prophet* by Kahlil Gibran, quoted in Chapter III. For the first time in thirty-eight years, she began to recognize her condition and the unhealthy character of her family relationships.

It takes the rare quality of a very mature person to stand firmly on two feet and accept the full responsibility for his own happiness. "In most marriages," says Dr. Murray Bowen, a founder of family psychotherapy and professor in the psychiatric department of Georgetown University, "the woman fuses her life style into that of her husband. Consequently, she loses her own identity. This can lead to marital conflict which occurs when neither spouse will give in to the other in the fusion, or when the one who has been giving in or adapting refuses to continue. The person who must do the adapting sometimes suffers from a physical or emotional illness or social dysfunction such as drinking or irresponsible behavior. Both husband and wife," Dr. Bowen continues, "must solve the problem by developing the 'Responsible I' approach in which both assume the burden of working toward his or her own happiness and comfort."

Once this concept is fully explored, understood, and applied, a miraculous change takes place in any couple's relationship. True love can exist only in an atmosphere of mutual respect and freedom. Each partner has to see the other as a whole person, worthy of respect and having the need to subscribe to his or her own identifiable self. Real togetherness can happen only when the two who are united can operate their minds and souls well apart.

There are hosts of dependencies. Parents are dependent on children and use them to gain emotional stability. Some children, like old dried leaves, cling past middle age to elderly parents. Some people switch dependencies from people to things, or to pets. Loving is freedom on both sides. Dependency is a fetter, binding and closing off the steam valves. A true self can't emerge when it's bottled up—unless it either explodes or is wisely let out, with caution, onto a predetermined route.

Dr. Bowen believes that the truly independent individual is one who can do his or her "own thing," while supporting and caring about others, too. Children shouldn't grow totally apart from parents. They should move on, independently and securely in life, keeping the family contacts warm and alive but not intertwined. While urging people to be responsible "I's," he sees the individual also as an integrated part of a whole family system. We are what we came from, and we are what we have progressed to be. You can't slough off the family and deny its effects. But you can stand on two firm feet and think and act on your own initiative.

"I am the most important person in my life," twenty-four-year-old Laurie Kendall said once. "My husband is second in importance to me and my children are also." She shocked a roomful of people with the statement, until she was able to make them understand exactly what it was she was saying. "Until I am secure in myself, and happy by myself, I can't contribute to the happiness of anyone else."

Only a person secure in his own identity can put aside the petty emotional trivia and get down to the business of living and letting live. In all personal relationships, dependency is the ball and chain. My first prescription for the relief of dependency is again from Gibran's *The Prophet.*

Then Almitra spoke again and said, "And what of Marriage,
Master?"
And he answered saying:
"You were born together, and together you shall be forever more.
You shall be together when the white wings of death scatter your
days.
Ay, you shall be together even in the silent memory of God.
But let there be spaces in your togetherness,
And let the winds of the heavens dance between you.

Love one another, but make not a bond of love:
Let it rather be a moving sea between the shores of your souls.
Fill each other's cup but drink not from one cup.
Give one another of your bread but eat not from the same loaf.
Sing and dance together and be joyous, but let each one of you
be alone,
Even as the strings of the lute are alone though they quiver with
the same music.

Give your hearts, but not into each other's keeping.
For only the hand of life can contain your hearts.
And stand together yet not too near together:
For the pillars of the temple stand apart,
And the oak tree and the cypress grow not in each other's
shadow."

Women have taken a stand today, as they have in the past, pro-
testing society's bonds, bonds that have made them lesser creatures
than their mates. The whole thought directed toward women has
been changing slowly, throughout time. There is no question about
it: our atmosphere has always been filled with a sense of women's
inferiority. The good wife, even in this enlightened age, is the one
who stays with the needs of the husband, home, and children and
seems to be fulfilled by them. Society has accepted the career
woman grudgingly. She, poor thing, can't be quite whole. Fortunately this attitude is changing. An Englishwoman, Anna Wick-
ham, who was born in 1884, struggled poetically against the restrictions of her role in the home. Her "Dedication of the Cook" is a
housewifely protest.

If any ask why there's no great she-poet,
Let him come live with me, and he will know it:
If I'd indite an ode or mend a sonnet,
I must go choose a dish or tie a bonnet;

For she who serves in forced virginity
Since I am wedded will not have me free;
And those new flowers my garden is so rich in
Must die for clammy odors of my kitchen.

Yet had I chosen Dian's barrenness
I'm not full woman, and I can't be less,
So could I state no certain truth for life,
Can I survive and be my good man's wife:

Yes! I will make the servant's cause my own
That she in pity leave me hours alone
So I will tend her mind and feed her wit
That she in time have her own joy of it;
And count it pride that not a sonnet's spoiled
Lacking her choice betwixt the baked and boiled.
So those young flowers my garden is so rich in
Will blossom from the ashes of my kitchen!

In a similar vein is a poem written by James Stephens called
"The Red Haired Man's Wife."

I have taken that vow—
And you were my friend
But yesterday—now
All that's at an end,
And you are my husband, and claim me, and I must depend.

Yesterday I was free,
Now you, as I stand,
Walk over to me
And take hold of my hand.
You look at my lips, your eyes are too bold, your smile is too
                                                                        bland.

My old name is lost,
My distinction of race,

Now the line has been crossed,
Must I step to your pace?
Must I walk as you list, and obey and smile up in your face?

All the white and the red
Of my cheeks you have won;
All the hair of my head,
And my feet, tho' they run,
Are yours, and you own me and end me just as I begun.

Must I bow when you speak,
Be silent and hear,
Inclining my cheek
And incredulous ear
To your voice, and command, and behest, hold your lightest
                                                     wish dear?

I am woman, but still
Am alive, and can feel
Every intimate thrill
That is woe or is weal.
I, aloof, and divided, apart, standing far, can I kneel?

If not, I shall know,
I shall surely find out.
And your world will throw
In disaster and rout;
I am woman and glory and beauty, I mystery, terror and doubt.

I am separate still,
I am I and not you,
And my mind and my will,
As in secret they grew,
Still are secret, unreached and untouched and not subject to
                                                     you.

Remember, these prescriptions are not intended to cure love!
They are only supposed to relieve the symptoms of dependency.
For, unless there is freedom in love, sooner or later there will be an
explosion. In a marriage, the slavery of dependency is not all on
the side of the female. Men are bound as tightly to their wedding

vows, and they can chaff as miserably also. The next prescription is by Rupert Brooke and is called "The Chilterns."

Your hands, my dear, adorable,
Your lips of tenderness
Oh, I've loved you faithfully and well,
Three years, or a bit less.
It wasn't a success.

Thank God, that's done! and I'll take the road,
Quit of my youth and you,
The Roman road to Wendover
By Tring and Lilley Hoo,
As a free man may do.

For youth goes over, the joys that fly,
The tears that follow fast;
And the dirtiest things we do must lie
Forgotten at the last;
Even love goes past.

What's left behind I shall not find,
The splendor and the pain;
The splash of sun, the shouting wind,
And the brave sting of rain,
I may not meet again.

Many of these poem prescriptions have been selected to show the problem and the pain of dependency. When it's recognized for what it is, it can be routed out and destroyed. Often one has to decide whether an action is the result of dependency, duty, or genuine devotion. What is it that causes a person, long after he is grown, to cling to parents, the old homestead, and even old memories? The next prescription is by D. H. Lawrence, whose dependency upon his mother is well recognized. The poem is called "Piano."

Softly in the dusk a woman is singing to me;
Taking me back down the vista of years, till I see
A child sitting under the piano, in the boom of the tingling

strings

Poetry for Peace of Mind

And pressing the small, poised feet of a mother who smiles as she
sings.

In spite of myself, the insidious mastery of song
Betrays me back, till the heart of me weeps to belong
To the old Sunday evenings at home, with winter outside
And hymns in the cosy parlor, the tinkling piano our guide.

So now it is vain for the singer to burst into clamor
With the great black piano appassionato. The glamour
Of childish days is upon me, my manhood is cast
Down the flood of remembrance, I weep like a child for the past.

I know of a child who worshiped her piano-playing father. She
used to crouch under the piano when he played, adoring him. He
died, suddenly, while she was still a child, and she was so bereft
and so dependent that she unconsciously took a negative independent stand. Without knowing it, she made a decision never to
let herself be so bound to another person again. Although she
married, she remained emotionally detached from her husband and
her children. Instead of relating to them, she fastened her dependencies securely to things, and made a fetish of her possessions.
While she appeared to be standing firm and independent, she
never really was. Actually she attached herself firmly to her
father's ghost, rejecting other relationships that could have been
healthy, independent, and joyful. "Soul's Liberty" by Anna Wick-
ham is a prescription for this invisible slavery.

He who has lost soul's liberty
Concerns himself forever with his property,
As, when the folk have lost both dance and song,
Women clean useless pots the whole day long.

Thank God for war and fire
To burn the silly objects of desire,
That from the ruin of a church thrown down
We see God clear and high above the town.

Fortunately for the newly born, parents instinctively have a
strong sense of responsibility during their infant years. Babies are

frail and vulnerable, and the interweaving is necessary for a while. An amusing, lighthearted prescription for dissolving the child-parent dependency at the right time is by Ogden Nash in "Song to Be Sung by the Father of Infant Female Children."

A heart leaps up when I behold
A rainbow in the sky;
Contrariwise, my blood runs cold
When little boys go by.
For little boys as little boys,
No special hate I carry,
But now and then they grow to men,
And when they do, they marry.
No matter how they tarry,
Eventually they marry.
And, swine among the pearls,
They marry little girls.

Oh, somewhere, somewhere, an infant plays,
With parents who feed and clothe him.
Their lips are sticky with pride and praise,
And I have begun to loathe him.
Yes, I loathe with a loathing shameless
This child who to me is nameless.
This bachelor child in his carriage
Gives never a thought to marriage,
But a person can hardly say knife
Before he will hunt him a wife.

I never see an infant (male)
A-sleeping in the sun,
Without I turn a trifle pale
And think, is he the one?
Oh, first he'll want to chop his curls,
And then he'll want a pony,
And then he'll think of pretty girls
And holy matrimony.
He'll put away his pony,
And sigh for matrimony.

A cat without a mouse
Is he without a spouse.

Oh, somewhere he bubbles, bubbles of milk,
And quietly sucks his thumbs;
His cheeks are roses painted on silk,
And his teeth are tucked in his gums.
But alas, the teeth will begin to grow,
And the bubbles will cease to bubble;
Given a score of years or so,
The roses will turn to stubble.
He'll sell a bond, or he'll write a book,
And his eyes will get that acquisitive look,
And raging and ravenous for the kill,
He'll boldly ask for the hand of Jill.
This infant whose middle
Is diapered still
Will want to marry
My daughter Jill.

Oh sweet be his slumber and moist his middle!
My dreams, I fear, are infanticiddle.
A fig for embryo Lohengrins!
I'll open all his safety pins,
I'll pepper his powder, and salt his bottle,
And give him readings from Aristotle.
Sand for his spinach I'll gladly bring,
And tabasco sauce for his teething ring.
Then perhaps he'll struggle through fire and water
To marry somebody *else's* daughter.

Once you take on Dr. Bowen's "Responsible I" attitude, the duties
and burdens of life ease. Much drudgery causes suffering because
it devalues the drudge. When you refuse to allow it to devalue you,
it turns into a job that must be done—but not one that will pin you
down in the position of a slave. There's a great increase in overall
happiness in the homes where both spouses decide to take the responsibility for their own happiness, and change their own images
of themselves from drudges to wholesome workers. When the bur-

den of drudgery lightens, it leaves more time for pursuit of interests that really count. The next prescription is by Louise Bogan and is called "Women."

Women have no wilderness in them,
They are provident instead,
Content in the tight hot cell of their hearts
To eat dusty bread.

They do not see cattle cropping red winter grass,
They do not hear
Snow water going down under culverts
Shallow and clear.

They wait, when they should turn to journeys,
They stiffen, when they should bend.
They use against themselves that benevolence
To which no man is friend.

They cannot think of so many crops to a field
Or of clean wood cleft by an ax.
Their love is an eager meaninglessness
Too tense, or too lax.

They hear in every whisper that speaks to them
A shout and a cry.
As like as not, when they take life over their door-sills
They should let it go by.

Each poem should point up the negatives of dependency and should encourage the shaking of its shackles. Try "The Solitary" by Sara Teasdale next.

My heart has grown rich with the passing of years,
I have less need now than when I was young
To share myself with every comer,
Or shape my thoughts into words with my tongue.

It is one to me that they come or go
If I have myself and the drive of my will,
And strength to climb on a summer night
And watch the stars swarm over the hill.

Let them think I love them more than I do,
Let them think I care, though I go alone,
If it lifts their pride, what is it to me,
Who am self-complete as a flower or a stone?

Add a dose or two of "The Slave" by James Oppenheim:

They set the slave free, striking off his chains . . .
Then he was as much of a slave as ever.

He was still chained to servility,
He was still manacled to indolence and sloth,
He was still bound by fear and superstition,
By ignorance, suspicion, and savagery . . .
His slavery was not in the chains,
But in himself. . . .

They can only set free men free . . .
And there is no need of that:
Free men set themselves free.

Wonderful Robert Frost has a dose for dependency in his poem "The Runaway."

Once when the snow of the year was beginning to fall,
We stopped by a mountain pasture to say, "Whose colt?"
A little Morgan had one forefoot on the wall,
The other curled at his breast. He dipped his head
And snorted to us. And then he had to bolt.
We heard the miniature thunder where he fled,
And we saw him, or thought we saw him, dim and gray,
Like a shadow against the curtain of falling flakes.
"I think the little fellow's afraid of the snow.
He isn't winter-broken. It isn't play
With the little fellow at all. He's running away.
I doubt if even his mother could tell him, 'Sakes,
It's only weather.' He'd think she didn't know!
Where is his mother? He can't be out alone."
And now he comes again with a clatter of stone
And mounts the wall again with whited eyes

And all his tail that isn't hair up straight.
He shudders his coat as if to throw off flies.
"Whoever it is that leaves him out so late,
When other creatures have gone to stall and bin,
Ought to be told to come and take him in."

Dependency is only right in infancy. Even handicapped people enrich their lives in proportion to how much they can learn in order to stand alone. I know a deaf woman who has never heard sound. She learned to speak and write and read, and takes tremendous pride in her ability to shop alone and run her household efficiently—alone. She has truly triumphed and made herself into an independent, responsible person.

Even the unborn infant struggles to be free. The following poem prescription, called "With Child," was written by Genevieve Taggard.

> Now I am slow and placid, fond of sun,
> Like a sleek beast, or a worn one:
> No slim and languid girl—not glad
> With the windy trip I once had,
> But velvet-footed, musing of my own,
> Torpid, mellow, stupid as a stone.
>
> You cleft me with your beauty's pulse, and now
> Your pulse has taken body. Care not how
> The old grace goes, how heavy I am grown,

Big with this loneliness, how you alone
Ponder our love. Touch my feet and feel
How earth tingles, teeming at my heel!

Earth's urge, not mine—my little death, not hers;
And the pure beauty yearns and stirs.
It does not heed our ecstasies, it turns
With secrets of its own, its own concerns,
Toward a windy world of its own, toward stark
And solitary places. In the dark,
Defiant even now, it tugs and moans
To be untangled from these mother's bones.

In the first chaotic crash of falling in love, dependency seems beautiful. Each person wants to live in the other's pocket for eternity, wrapped in the edges of the pink cloud they float upon. As the marriage relationship matures and deepens, the partners find that they can and *must* also stand alone. If they are too fused, to use Dr. Bowen's term, breaking apart is painful and, sometimes, can't be done. The following prescription for separate-togetherness by Marya Zaturenska is called "The Lovers."

My glittering sky, high, clear, profound,
Be thou my alps, I'll be thy summer.
I'll be thy summer and the ground
Where all thy garlands, all thy honors found
In the sky's mirror, fire and dew contend,
Which shall excel, which shall transcend.

Be thou my mountain heights, I'll be the plain,
Warm, simple, sweet, complaisant to the rain,
Complaisant to the rain and wind, the common day.
I'll be the daisy field where happy children play,
Where happy children play, where the world's voice is heard
In a tree, in the grass, in the storm, in a bird.

Be thou the diamond water-crisp, and I the fire
Rosy and quick within the ruby's flame,
Within the ruby's flame inscribe my name
Sensitive on the spirit's delicate wire,

Send occult messages no human tongue can say.
Be thou the night, I'll be the day.

I'll be the day, so fresh, so morning bright,
And thy youth's dawning and the fields of light,
The fields of light that change dark to bright.
Thou my tranquillity, I thy delight,
Thou the thin light of opals on my wrist
And I the evening-tinted heaven brooding amethyst.

Be thou the waterbuck and I the hart
Drinking in coolness from rain-moistened heat,
Drinking in coolness where the willows part,
And where the willows part, two diverse shadows meet.
Be thou the sheltered pool, and I the busy street
And we the shades that one another meet.

Change then forever, be forever the same,
Who have one road, one destiny, one name,
One destiny, one name, jewel, dew, fire (never the same),
The mountain and the river, city and plain.
Separate, distinct, divided, parted, meeting ever
What the eye loses, let the heart recover.

Sir Thomas Wootton, writing in the sixteenth and seventeenth centuries, produced my last tiny capsule of a poem prescription. It's the utmost in marital dependency, and is called, "Upon the Death of Sir Albert Morton's Wife."

> He first deceased; she for a little tried
> To live without him, liked it not, and died.

XIV

Anxiety

10¢ 25 shots

※

Anxiety is that black gnawing feeling in the middle of your stomach. It has no relationship to reality or genuine fear and can attack at any time. It can happen when you are most secure; money in the bank, perfect health, children all at home in bed, when suddenly, your nerves start to crawl and there you are, feeling anxious or apprehensive.

Growing up is the most difficult thing a human being does. We grow up, learning to see ourselves as others have drawn us. Parents make one portrait of us, teachers another, and our friends a third. A chance statement makes a lifetime impression. "Someone said once that I had nice eyes," Eve said. "I never forgot it."

Marianne's family thought it amusing to say that Marianne was a "nit-wit." She grew up with the conviction that she had no intelligence, that her brain was lightweight, and that she should avoid any "heavy" thinking. No one ever grew up without some of the lines of the portrait having been drawn by a variety of artists. In time we come to accept a total image. Then if we step outside that image, even if it is only for a moment, anxiety attacks. Subconsciously we feel that we have defied the "authorities" who shaped us.

The woman I mentioned in another chapter, who *dared* to step out of her image and learn to sing, is an example. Having been told all her growing years that she *couldn't* sing, that she was tone-deaf, it was impossible for her to defy the ghosts of the past without some symptoms of anxiety. Anxiety attacks when the thing you *dare* to do is being done successfully.

I was told as a child that I was hopelessly poor at languages. I struggled with French later in life, when I was preparing for a trip to Europe. I had no attacks of anxiety over the resulting increased knowledge of the language, because my skill didn't increase substantially. I still felt that my accent was terrible and that basically I had no ability to learn a language. Had I been highly successful in my efforts, I probably would have been stricken with anxiety.

Margaret was told as a child that she was the family's ugly duckling. Her parents used to say, stupidly, that her sister Joan was the beauty and that Margaret had the brains. Margaret spent a lifetime coping with attacks of anxiety because circumstances kept pointing out the fact that her family's statement was not really true. It took her a long time to learn that she didn't have to stay within the mold her parents had cast.

You must come to terms with what you are, as opposed to what others have said you were. Anxiety must be put down fiercely, as one would put down a charging dog. It is entirely possible to change your self-image. It takes work, but it's worth it. You have to stand back and look at yourself objectively and admit your right to be what you really are. Poetry helps immensely. Whatever your state and whoever you are, there is strength in knowing that the poet struggled with the same confusions, doubts, and fears. The problem with any emotion is the strange singularity it seems to have; it acts as though it belonged solely to you. Poetry proves the universality of all the feelings that plague mankind. My first prescription for anxiety is "A Vagrant" by Erik Axel Karlfeldt, translated by Charles Wharton Stork.

> "Who are you and whence do you come?"
> I will not and can not reply,
> I am no man's son and I have no home,
> No son shall I leave when I die.
> A stranger from far am I.
>
> "What's your religion, what is your creed?"
> I only know this: I know naught.

And if I have missed the right path, indeed
My error I've never been taught.
But God first and last I have sought.

"How is your life?" It is storm and pain,
A hard, endless battle-drive;
A glow that is quenched, a hope made vain,
And clouds that with sunbeams strive,
But still I am glad I'm alive.

It takes the same kind of courage to deal with anxiety that stems from no apparent cause as it does to deal with fear. In either case, you simply have to face the lion and subdue him. In "Waste Places" by James Stephen there is a prescription for dealing with anxiety.

As a naked man I go
Through the desert, sore afraid;
Holding high my head, although
I'm as frightened as a maid.

The lion crouches there! I saw
In barren rocks his amber eye!
He parts the cactus with his paw!
He stares at me as I go by!

He would pad upon my trace
If he thought I was afraid!
If he knew my hardy face
Veils the terrors of a maid.

He rises in the night-time, and
He stretches forth! He snuffs the air!
He roars! He leaps along the sand!
He creeps! He watches everywhere!

His burning eyes, his eyes of bale
Through the darkness I can see!
He lashes fiercely with his tail!
He makes again to spring at me!

I am the lion, and his lair!
I am the fear that frightens me!

I am the desert of despair!
And the night of agony!

Night or day, whate'er befall,
I must walk that desert land,
Until I dare my fear and call
The lion out to lick my hand.

Along the same metaphoric lines is a prescription by Ogden Nash: "The Adventures Of Isabel."

Isabel met an enormous bear;
Isabel, Isabel, didn't care.
The bear was hungry, the bear was ravenous,
The bear's big mouth was cruel and cavernous.
The bear said, Isabel, glad to meet you,
How do, Isabel, now I'll eat you!
Isabel, Isabel, didn't worry;
Isabel didn't scream or scurry.
She washed her hands and she straightened her hair up,
Then Isabel quietly ate the bear up.

Once on a night as black as pitch
Isabel met a wicked old witch.
The witch's face was cross and wrinkled,
The witch's gums with teeth were sprinkled.
Ho, ho, Isabel! the old witch crowed,
I'll turn you into an ugly toad!
Isabel, Isabel, didn't worry;
Isabel didn't scream or scurry.
She showed no rage and she showed no rancor,
But she turned the witch into milk and drank her.

Isabel met a hideous giant,
Isabel continued self-reliant,
The giant was hairy, the giant was horrid,
He had one eye in the middle of his forehead.
Good morning, Isabel, the giant said,
I'll grind your bones to make my bread.
Isabel, Isabel, didn't worry;

Isabel didn't scream or scurry.
She nibbled the zwieback that she always fed off,
And when it was gone, she cut the giant's head off.

Isabel met a troublesome doctor,
He punched and poked till he really shocked her.
The doctor's talk was one of coughs and chills,
And the doctor's satchel bulged with pills.
The doctor said unto Isabel,
Swallow this, it will make you well.
Isabel, Isabel, didn't worry;
Isabel didn't scream or scurry.
She took those pills from the pill-concoctor,
And Isabel calmly cured the doctor.

As children, we faced a barrage of no's. Until the age of reason (whenever that is) we seemed constantly to be interested in doing only those things that adults didn't want us to do. Finally we learned that something unpleasant, like a spanking, occurred when we tried forbidden things. The results of some of these actions must have carried into adulthood. We aren't conscious of it, of course, but memory stirs invisibly within us whenever we try something new. Children struggle within themselves much more than their parents think they do. Sully Prudhomme has a prescription for anxiety in "The Struggle," translated by Arthur O'Shaughnessy.

Nightly tormented by returning doubt,
I dare the sphinx with faith and unbelief;
And through lone hours when no sleep brings relief
The monster rises all my hopes to flout.
In a still agony, the light blown out,
I wrestle with the unknown; nor long nor brief
The night appears, my narrow couch of grief
Grown like the grave with Death walled around about.
Sometimes my mother, coming with her lamp,
Seeing my brow as with a death-sweat damp,
Asks, "Ah, what ails thee, Child? Hast thou no rest?"
And then I answer, touched by her look of yearning,

Holding my beating heart and forehead burning,
"Mother, I strove with God, and was hard prest."

Most of us think less of ourselves than we should. Much anxiety comes from the struggle to be something other than what we are. Two prescriptions for the result of such anxiety follow. The first is "The Blade of Grass" by Stephen Crane.

> In Heaven
> Some little blades of grass
> Stood before God.
> "What did you do?"
> Then all save one of the little blades
> Began eagerly to relate
> The merits of their lives.
> This one stayed a small way behind,
> Ashamed.
>
> Presently, God said,
> "And what did you do?"
> The little blade answered, "Oh, my Lord,
> Memory is bitter to me,
> For if I did good deeds,
> I know not of them."
> Then God, in all his splendor,
> Arose from his throne.
> "Oh, best little blade of grass!" He said.

The second prescription is Polonius' advice to Laertes from *Hamlet* by William Shakespeare.

> There,—my blessing with you!
> And these few precepts in thy memory
> See thou character. Give thy thoughts no tongue,
> Nor any unproportion'd thought his act.
> Be thou familiar, but by no means vulgar.
> The friends thou hast, and their adoption tried,
> Grapple them to thy soul with hoops of steel;

But do not dull thy palm with entertainment
Of each new-hatched, unfledged comrade. Beware
Of entrance to a quarrel; but being in,
Bear't that the opposed may beware of thee,
Give every man thine ear, but few thy voice:
Take each man's censure, but reserve thy judgement.
Costly thy habit as thy purse can buy,
But not expressed in fancy; rich, not gaudy:
For the apparel oft proclaims the man.
Neither a borrower nor a lender be,
For loan oft loses both itself and friend,
And borrowing dulls the edge of husbandry.
This above all: to thine own self be true,
And it must follow, as the night the day,
Thou canst not then be false to any man.

For centuries, there has been a kind of Puritan thinking that to be humble and self-deprecating is to be good. Some lusty individuals such as Walt Whitman have protested the importance of a good self-image; but in general the Pilgrim self-effacer has always been looked upon as possessing desirable characteristics. Yet, as Shakespeare knew, man must be true to himself in order to be true to anyone else. Walt Whitman's "Song of the Open Road" is a vibrant, powerful antidote for the poison of anxiety.

Afoot and light-hearted I take to the open road,
Healthy, free, the world before me,
The long brown path before me leading wherever I choose.
Henceforth I ask not good-fortune, I myself am good-fortune,
Henceforth I whimper no more, postpone no more, need nothing.
Done with indoor complaints, libraries, querulous criticisms,
Strong and content I travel the open road.

The earth, that is sufficient,
I do not want the constellations any nearer,
I know they are very well where they are,
I know they suffice for those who belong to them.

I think heroic deeds were all conceiv'd in the open air, and all
        free poems also.

I think I could stop here myself and do miracles.

I think whatever I shall meet on the road I shall like, and whoever beholds me shall like me.

I think whoever I see must be happy.

From this hour I ordain myself loos'd of limits and imaginary lines,

Going where I list, my own master total and absolute,

Listening to others, considering well what they say,

Pausing, searching, receiving, contemplating,

Gently, but with undeniable will, divesting myself of the holds that would hold me.

I inhale great draughts of space,

The east and the west are mine, and the north and the south are mine.

I am larger, better than I thought.

I did not know I had so much goodness.

Now if a thousand perfect men were to appear it would not amaze me,

Now if a thousand beautiful forms of women appear'd it would not astonish me.

Now I see the secret of the makings of the best persons,

It is to grow in the open air, and to eat and sleep with the earth.

Listen! I will be honest with you,

I do not offer the old smooth prizes, but offer rough new prizes,

These are the days that must happen to you:

You shall not heap up what is called riches,

You shall scatter with lavish hand all that you earn or achieve,

You but arrive at the city to which you were destined, you hardly settle yourself to satisfaction before you are called by an irresistible call to depart,

You shall be treated to the ironical smiles and mockings of those who remain behind you,

What beckonings of love you receive you shall only answer with passionate kisses of parting,

You shall not allow the hold of those who spread their reach'd hands toward you.

Allons! the road is before us!
It is safe—I have tried it—my own feet have tried it well—Be not
detain'd!
Let the paper remain on the desk unwritten, and the book on
the shelf unopen'd!
Let the tools remain in the workshop! Let the money remain
unearn'd!
Let the school stand! mind not the cry of the teacher!
Let the preacher preach in his pulpit! Let the lawyer plead in
the court, and the judge expound the law.

Camerado, I give you my hand!
I give you my love more precious than money,
I give you myself before preaching or law;
Will you give me yourself? will you come travel with me?
Shall we stick by each other as long as we live?

There is never only one panacea. All problems have several
solutions. When you read poetry you benefit from the rhythms, the
sounds, the messages. Walt Whitman's suggestion that you take to
the open road is a good one. A return to nature is a return to a
healthy source. "One Beauty Still" is prescription by George
Dillon.

> One beauty still is faultless, not
> Deflowered in the bed of thought:
> It is a sound of sunken seas.
> It is an avid wish for ease.
> It is the earth, it is the sky
> When passion is a lute put by,
> And life is a dancer out of breath.
> It is the lovely face of death,
> Adored and guessed at—never once
> Beheld in chrysoprase or bronze;
> Not in the temple or the grove,
> Not in a hundred nights of love.
>
> This was the morning sun, the wild
> Day break of anguish in the child.

This is the sun at noon no less,
Deep in the dome of nothingness.
Wherefore, impoverished heart, be proud
To wear the purple of the shroud:
If you are friendless, take for friend
The noble wave, the affluent wind.
If you are homeless, do not care:
Inhabit the bright house of air.
If you are worn with wayfaring,
Lie down within the arms of spring.

If you really want a potent dose for any ailment, take these prescriptions outdoors, by a brook, by the ocean, or on top of a mountain—and let them go to work on you! Take a dose of "The Hills" by Frances Cornford.

Out of the complicated house, come I
To walk beneath the sky.
Here mud and stones and turf, here everything
Is mutely comforting.
Now hung upon the twigs and thorns appear
A host of lovely rain-drops cold and clear.
And on the bank
Or deep in brambly hedges dank
The small birds nip about and say:
"Brothers, the Spring is not so far away!"
The hills like mother-giantesses old
Lie in the cold,
And with a complete patience, let
The cows come cropping on their bosoms wet,
And even tolerate that such as I
Should wander by
With paltry leathern heel which cannot harm
Their bodies' calm,
And, with a heart they cannot know, to bless
The enormous power of their peacefulness.

The last prescription for the easing of anxiety is by William Ellery Leonard. It's called "To the Victor."

Man's mind is larger than his brow of tears;
This hour is not my all of time: this place
My all of earth; nor this obscene disgrace
My all of life; and thy complacent sneers
Shall not pronounce my doom to my compeers
While the hereafter lights me in the face,
And from the past, as from the mountain's base,
Rise, as I rise, the long tumultuous cheers.
And who slays me must overcome a world:
Heroes at arms, and virgins who became
Mothers of children, prophecy and song;
Walls of old cities with their flags unfurled;
Peaks, headlands, ocean and its isles of fame—
And sun and moon and all that made me strong!

XV
Adolescence

Adolescence is a strange malady that occurs when the adult and the child within a person are each struggling for existence. It is a time of unprecedented miseries, inexplicable joys, and intolerable confusions. It is a time of awakening to the world and to the potential of one's own mind that creates tremendous yearnings that swiftly move from concern for suffering children in Pakistan to concern for the state of one's own heart in regard to the boy or girl next door. Never having tested thoughts against experience, the adolescent feels too intensely. Everything that enters his range of emotion is of massive importance. As he begins to understand his position in the universe, it both terrifies and thrills him. Meanwhile he strangely feels his own developing body, soul, and mind and doesn't know where to place them in relation to his universal post.

Almost invariably he comes in conflict with his parents. Until puberty, he had been a charming and obliging child, past the perversities of infancy, and a warm, loving, and lovable human. Overnight he becomes a startling enigma. Parents find it hard to realize and accept the fact that he must fight them to be free. They forget how it was when they were young. As they become adult, children have to rebel. Otherwise, it would be too easy to remain in their cocoons. Demands are placed on young people to make decisions about college, a career, about life. They have discovered that they will be required to take their places in adult society, make decisions in the community, vote for a president, behave responsibly, perhaps marry and rear their own children. It's a bewildering and frightening situation.

The only way they can make a genuine, healthy break with family ties is through a firm, albeit subconscious, rebellion. By creating an intolerable home and family situation, the child forces his way to freedom. Having established himself as an adult, he can return with affection and pleasure to the family; that is, if the parents don't alienate themselves from him during the struggle.

A large percentage of young people turn passionately to poetry in the transition from their childhood days to adulthood. A seventeen-year-old boy in Canaan, Connecticut, walked sixteen miles to Torrington and back one night just to hear the late Mark Van Doren read his poems. Parents, teachers, and bookstore proprietors report a surge to the classics (as well as the modern) by young people during their early high school years. They retain it too. The visiting-poet circuits are rewardingly well attended, with teens and college students leading the big parade.

Arthur Hagadus, proprietor of the Hickory Stick Book Shop in Washington Depot, Connecticut, has told me that paperbacks sell overwhelmingly to teens.

David Silverstein in Lennox, Massachusetts, says young people invade his store, buying E. E. Cummings, Dylan Thomas, and the so-called "young" poets such as Richard Brautigan.

Mr. Hagadus also says that styles and preferences for poets change from year to year. "Each group needs its very own poet. They have to identify with someone they consider their own."

I wouldn't presume to invade the privacy of the adolescent reader and select something that will help him find peace during his struggle to grow. My poem prescriptions to bridge the gap between adolescence and maturity are only a smattering of some that have been known to help, inspire, and excite young people in groups with whom I have worked, and I hope they will be the inspiration for a more thorough search for the rewards of poetry.

Writing poetry helps the teen therapeutically too, and some of the offerings are magnificently good. Here, for example, is one by a high school junior, Gail Killens, at Mount St. Joseph's Academy in West Hartford, Connecticut. It was published in the school's literary annual, *Fontes,* in 1968. It's called "Boy from Tennessee."

All alone. . . . .
Khe Sahn, outpost. . . . .
Beyond the barbed wire;
First intelligence mission,
Black boy from Tennessee.
"What did you do all night long,
Boy from Tennessee?"
"I prayed just about all the time,"
Said the boy from Tennessee.
"What did you think of, may I ask,
Young boy from Tennessee?"
"I thought, Dawn keep coming:
Keep coming on,"
Said the boy from Tennessee.

Two more poems by a teen are written by Jacqueline M. Fitz-gerald, also of Hartford. The first is called "Two and the Sea."

O, we must visit the sea again
Before the tide comes in,
To find our footprints in the sand,
To walk again, hand in hand,
Before the tide comes in.

For when the tide begins to rise
Up to the rocks above,
The sun, the fish and gulls all know
It's time for us to go—
To leave the place we love.

Whatever Jackie specifically had in mind, of course, is something that only she knows; but in her poem I feel some of the adolescent struggle toward maturity—some of the strain toward the world that occurs in a teen when the tide comes in and washes out childish footprints and moves him from the closeness and security of home. In her next poem Jackie expresses some of the anger and frustration with adults that make the young rebellious. It's called "The Wordy People."

With spectacles set firmly upon the nose
And lethal dictionary in hand,
This busy scholar uses every opportunity
To disguise the meaning of his minute pen-scratchings.
Mental giant is his self image,
A god of the pen,
A master of prefixed and suffixed words
Sitting at his desk
Creating literary monsters
Which threaten to obliterate true artistry.
In painful wordiness,
He turns out manuscripts of meaningless groups of words.
The light burns unceasingly in his study,
Revealing—at the most,
A shadow. . . . .
    of a man.

Adolescence is a problem in two ways. It intensely and seriously
affects concerned parents as well as the youth going through it.
Parents need understanding and support, too, during the maturing
crisis. They certainly won't receive it from their young; the perspec-
tives on both sides are too distorted. Nor is there a doctor who can
effect a cure. Counseling surely helps, either from a friend who
has weathered the adolescent storm with her own or, preferably,
from a professional. For the most part, however, it's a time and
condition that needs only to be lived down. The poem prescriptions
that follow have been chosen to help parents as well as the teen to
"live it down." The first is one of the most beautiful youth-maturity-
struggle poems that has ever been written. It is from the pen of a
great poet who thought upon the subject overmuch, but never quite
made the transition himself. Here is "Fern Hill" by Dylan Thomas.

Now as I was young and easy under the apple boughs
About the lilting house and happy as the grass was green,
The night above the dingle starry.
Time let me hail and climb
Golden in the heydays of his eyes,
And honored among wagons I was prince of the apple towns

And once below a time I lordly had the trees and leaves
Trail with daisies and barley
Down the rivers of the windfall light.

And as I was green and carefree, famous among the barns
About the happy yard and singing as the farm was home,
In the sun that is young once only,
Time let me play and be
Golden in the mercy of his means,
And green and golden I was huntsman and herdsman, the calves
Sang to my horn, the foxes on the hills barked clear and cold
And the sabbath rang slowly
In the pebbles of the holy streams.

All the sun long it was running, it was lovely, the hay-
Fields high as the house, the tunes from the chimneys, it was air
And playing, lovely and watery
And fire green as grass.
And nightly under the simple stars
As I rode to sleep the owls were bearing the farm away,
All the moon long I heard, blessed among stables, the night jars
Flying with the ricks, and the horses
Flashing into the dark.

And then to awake, and the farm, like a wanderer white
With the dew, come back, the cock on his shoulder: it was all
Shining, it was Adam and maiden,
The sky gathered again
And the sun grew round that very day.
So it must have been after the birth of the simple light
In the first, spinning place, the spellbound horses walking warm
Out of the whinnying stable
On to the fields of praise.

And honored among foxes and pheasants by the gay house
Under the new made clouds and happy as the heart was long,
In the sun born over and over.
I ran my heedless ways,
My wishes raced through the house-high hay
And nothing I cared, at my sky blue trades, that time allows

In all his tuneful turning so few and such golden songs
Before the children green and golden
Follow him out of grace.

Nothing I cared, in the lamb white days, that time would take
        me
Up to the swallow thronged left by the shadow of my hand,
In the moon that is always rising,
Nor that riding to sleep
I should hear him fly with the high fields
And wake to the farm forever fled from the childless land,
Oh as I was young and easy in the mercy of his means,
Time held me green and dying
Though I sang in my chains like the sea.

As a prescription, Dylan Thomas has to be taken over and over, preferably out loud. There's a unique and tenderly beautiful sound and sense to his language that only reveals itself as you absorb it.

The discovery of love possesses the young. It's one of the first great discoveries in the new adult and when it happens, it seems to those involved like the first such feeling ever felt in the history of man. Here are two prescriptions by A. E. Housman, a poet to whom youth have long related. The first is "When I Was One-and-Twenty."

> When I was one-and-twenty
> I heard a wise man say,
> "Give crowns and pounds and guineas
> But not your heart away;
> Give pearls away and rubies
> But keep your fancy free."
> But I was one-and-twenty,
> No use to talk to me.
>
> When I was two-and-twenty
> I heard him say again,
> "The heart out of the bosom
> Was never given in vain;
> 'Tis paid with sighs a plenty

And sold for endless rue."
And I am two-and-twenty,
And oh, 'tis true, 'tis true.

Now the second: "Oh, When I Was in Love with You":

> Oh, when I was in love with you,
> Then I was clean and brave,
> And miles around the wonder grew
> How well did I behave.
>
> And now the fancy passes by,
> And nothing will remain,
> And miles around they'll say that I
> Am quite myself again.

"In the Time of 'The Breaking of Nations'" by Thomas Hardy goes well with the two foregoing poems.

> Only a man harrowing clods
> In a slow silent walk
> With an old horse that stumbles and nods
> Half asleep as they stalk.
>
> Only thin smoke without flame
> From the heaps of couch-grass;
> Yet this will go onward the same
> Though Dynasties pass.
>
> Yonder a maid and her wight
> Come whispering by:
> War's annals will fade into night
> Ere their story die.

The so-called "young poets" have managed a magnificent rapport with teens today. They may come and go in status with the young as each teen generation moves forward, as Arthur Hagadus pointed out, but they serve them well none the less. One of the most successful was, and I believe still is, Richard Brautigan. Two prescriptions for bridging adolescence are from his book *The Pill Versus the Spring Hill Mine Disaster*. The first is called "It's Raining in Love."

I don't know what it is,
But I distrust myself
When I start to like a girl
A lot.

It makes me nervous.
I don't say the right things
Or perhaps I start
To examine, evaluate, compute
What I am saying.

If I say, "Do you think it is going to rain?"
And she says "I don't know,"
I start thinking: Does she really like me?

In other words
I get a little creepy.

A friend of mine once said,
"It's twenty times better to be friends
With someone
Than it is to be in love with them."
I think he's right and besides,
It's raining somewhere, programming flowers
And keeping snails happy.
That's all taken care of.

BUT

If a girl likes me a lot
And starts getting real nervous
And suddenly begins asking me funny questions
And looks sad if I give the wrong answers
And she says things like,
"Do you think it is going to rain?"
And I say, "It beats me,"

And she says, "Oh,"
And looks a little sad
At the clear blue California sky,
I think: Thank God, it's you, Baby, this time
Instead of me.

The second Brautigan poem prescription is "Gee, You're So Beautiful That It's Starting to Rain."

Oh, Marcia,
I want your long blond beauty
To be taught in high school,
So kids will learn that God
Lives like music in the skin
And sounds like a sunshine harpsichord.
I want high school report cards
To look like this:

Playing with Gentle Glass Things
A

Computer Magic
A

Writing Letters To Those You Love
A

Finding Out About Fish
A

Marcia's long blond beauty
A Plus!

My next and last prescription for adolescence comes to us from Robert Frost. It's called "Into My Own."

One of my wishes is that those dark trees,
So old and firm they scarcely know the breeze,
Were not, as 'twere, the merest mask of gloom,
But stretched away unto the edge of doom.

I should not be withheld but that some day
Into their vastness I should steal away,
Fearless of ever finding open land,
Or highways where the slow wheel pours the sand.

I do not see why I should e'er turn back,
Or those should not set forth upon my track
To overtake me, who should miss me here
And long to know if I still hold them dear.

They would not find me changed from him they knew—
Only more sure of all I thought was true.

Bridging adolescence is a problem for both the adolescent and his elders. Both reading and writing poetry is therapeutic, and the two following poems are mine, written at a time when I was trying to survive the teen years of my two daughters. The first one is called "Captive Bird."

She crouched into my palm
The tiny beat of startled heart
Murmuring to my flesh.
Herself, made small for her defense.
My large hand held her captive, frail and tense,
A light and winged mystery, wild art.
Stroked I the simple silver of her spine
And laid my fingers open, setting free
The softness of her cowered dependency.
Touched by her faith in me, and kind,
I laid her on the wind and let it hold
Her buoyant softness on the guardian air.
She felt her liberation press her there
And coasted to a tree, myself behind.

I turned and saw my daughter's growing face
Match freedoms blend with my restrictions loose.
I didn't tell her how it troubled me.
It wouldn't really have been any use.

The second poem is called "On the Edge."

She had no choice.
There was nowhere for her to grow
But up.
Otherwise she would have remained a child,
And stayed on the beach in Maine.
Not forbidding duty,
Or those market hands of mischief
That make a breathless child into
A holder of possessions.
She possessed.
The beach in Maine was hers,
And with it she held to her duty
To test infinity.
The force of time was pushing from the sea
And the waves tried to drown out the growing sound:
All the sand, salt, sea-bird sounds of summer.
They tried to keep her there a child,
But she had no choice.
There was nowhere for her to grow
But up.

Time passes and poetry remains. This is one of the therapeutic truths of poetry. For centuries the minds of thinkers, philosophers, and dreamers have been recording their observations on paper in the finest language they could muster. How comforting it is to know that everything we deal with inside ourselves has been dealt with since written history began! I have no more prescriptions for adolescence. I found too many to possibly use, and I repeat—each teen should search out his own. And parents should encourage them in their search. Of all the emotional problems that beset us, growing up needs direction toward poetry because it's instinctive for the young to turn to it for solace, the solace we often turn away from after we have matured.

The first sounds of comfort the infant knows come from the beat of its mother's heart. Babies don't have to be taught to respond to rhythm; they just do. Small children don't have to be taught to chant as they jump rope and play sidewalk games; they just do. Preschoolers are captivated by the sound and feeling of poetry read to them in the form of nursery rhymes. It's natural that they resort to such an innately human thing as poetry when they face their first real crisis—at the edge of maturity.

Poetry for Peace of Mind

EPILOGUE

Someone once said that there are only four real emotions and that everything else is a result or offshoot of them. This may well be. The poetry I have selected is for the relief of symptoms as we know them. The fact that these prescriptions work has been proven in hospitals across the country, in Canada, in Russia, and throughout the world. If poems serve to relieve the ailments of the truly sick, then think what they can do for you!

I hope you'll continue to pursue anthologies and collections, searching for those special, instantly recognizable, personal poems that immediately relate to you and your mood or condition of the moment. Once you have truly made the world's great poets your friends, you have a solid buffer against loneliness and all other griefs and frustrations of man.

Man is language. It is him throughout the ages, speaking of the crisis and conflicts, the triumphs and disasters, the love and dissolutions, the fear and the pain and the joy. Without language to relate these things, we would never have walked on the moon. The majesty of what mortals have done deserves telling in the finest and most majestic of language, with simplicity and concern. Those who have achieved this language are our poets.

INDEX OF TITLES

INDEX OF FIRST LINES

INDEX OF AUTHORS

Alison Wyrley Birch

POETRY FOR PEACE OF MIND

"Come read to me some poem,
Some simple and heartfelt lay,
That shall soothe this restless
feeling,
And banish the thoughts of day."

from "The Day Is Done"
—by Henry Wadsworth Longfellow

We all have moments of depression, anxiety, loneliness, or just plain boredom. Sometimes, the right words spoken or read at the right time can help us to get in touch with our feelings and even overcome them. And the words of the great poets can have a healing power all their own.

Today, poetry therapy is being used by psychiatrists all over the country. In this unique book, Alison Wyrley Birch, a poet herself, has arranged some of her favorite verses according to their emotional impact so that you can be your own "poetry therapist"—